MYTHS
AND
LEGENDS

MYTHS
AND
LEGENDS

Grange
BOOKS

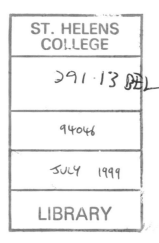
A QUANTUM BOOK

Published by Grange Books
An imprint of Grange Books plc
The Grange
Grange Yard
London SE1 3AG

ISBN 1-85627-915-4

This book was produced by
Quantum Books Ltd
6 Blundell Street
London N7 9BH

Creative Director: Peter Bridgewater
Art Director: Terry Jeavons
Designer: Sally McKay
Project Editor: Caroline Beattie
Editor: Susan Baker
Picture Researcher: Jon Newman
Illustrator: Lorraine Harrison

Typeset in Great Britain by
Central Southern Typesetters, Eastbourne
Manufactured in Hong Kong
by Eray Scan Pte. Ltd
Printed and bound in Singapore by
Star Standard Industries

The material in this book previously appeared in
An Introduction to Viking Mythology
An Introduction to Greek Mythology and
An Introduction to Oriental Mythology

CONTENTS

VIKING
MYTHOLOGY

Tales of Gods
and Goddesses

LEFT *Nineteenth-
century book
illustration depicting
Aegir, god of the sea,
and his wife Ran, who
used her net to snatch
sailors from the decks
of their ships.*

AEGIR AND NJORD

BELOW *Viking sword pommel found in Sweden and now in the National Museum of Antiquities, Stockholm. This could date from about the tenth century.*

Both Aegir and Njord were gods of the sea; the former was one of the Aesir (if not a member of an even earlier family of gods) and the latter one of the Vanir. In the early days the Norse worshipped Aegir and nodded their heads towards Njord; later they worshipped Njord and barely remembered Aegir as a separate god. During this time the stories of Aegir and Njord became inextricably mixed up with each other. Since the sea was so important to the Vikings, the whole process represented a fairly significant turnaround.

Aegir lived in a hall beneath the sea near the island of Hlesey. He shared the hall with his wife-sister, Ran. Much hated, Ran was the goddess of death for all who perished at sea. Her task was to use a net to haul men from the decks of ships to a watery grave in the hall she shared with her husband-brother. One legend has it that mariners might reappear at their own funeral feasts if Ran had welcomed them to the seafloor with especial enthusiasm. And, even for those less fortunate, her welcome was not neces-

sarily unfriendly: in her seafloor hall the mead flowed as freely as it did at Valhalla, and couches were set out to receive the bodies of the drowned. Sailors who went overboard bearing gold were particularly well received; Ran loved gold, and used its gleam to illuminate the submarine hall. Ran and Aegir had nine beautiful giantess daughters, the Wave Maidens, with whom Odin mated to produce (from all the mothers simultaneously) the god Heimdall.

Aegir himself was one of the brothers of Loki and Kari. He, too, seems to have been unpopular among the Vikings, because of his perceived delight in swooping over the tops of the waves to capsize ships and seize their crews.

Once Aegir and Ran were relaxing in their hall when Thor and Tyr burst in. The gods of Asgard had run out of mead: Thor demanded that Aegir and Ran should swiftly do some brewing to end this shortage. Aegir was not best pleased by Thor's demand, but said that he would try his hardest if Thor could only produce a cauldron or kettle large enough for Aegir to brew sufficient of the stuff. The god replied that this would be no problem, and Tyr chipped in to mention that his father, the giant Hymir, possessed a suitably huge cauldron. Thor and Tyr went to the home of Hymir but found that he wasn't there; instead there were two women. One of these was Tyr's grandmother, now transmuted into a hag with 900 heads. The other was Tyr's mother, and was lovely; she brought the two gods mugs of ale and suggested that, after they'd drunk it, they should conceal themselves under a pair of Hymir's cauldrons; she warned them that his glance was so powerful that it could kill. Almost immediately afterwards, Hymir entered his hall, looking around with a venomous gaze; all of the rafters split except, fortunately, the one that had been supporting the cauldrons hanging over the two gods. Hymir welcomed his visitors and gave them food, killing three cows, two of which Thor ate. The giant was

RIGHT *Nineteenth-century book ilillustration representing Njord and Skadi on their way from Asgard to Noatûn after their honeymoon.*

somewhat upset by this, and told Thor that the following morning they would go fishing together, using their own bait. Thor responded by chopping of the head of one of Hymir's cattle, Himinibrioter, to use as a bait.

The god and the giant rowed out to sea. Thor was looking for the Midgard Snake (Jormungand), and frequently he dipped his fingers beneath the boat to search for it. Even though he had the bull's head, the god was unsuccessful; Hymir, on the other hand, fetched up two whales. Then Thor caught the Midgard Snake, stretching his feet against the base of the ship. His feet went right through, and the giant panicked: he cut the line so that the snake sank back to the depths of the ocean.

Thor, infuriated, hit Hymir with his hammer. The giant was fortunately unharmed and the two of them waded ashore: Thor carried the boat they had been sailing in while the giant carried his two whales. They shared the whales for breakfast. Then the god attempted to prove his strength by throwing a pewter beaker against the giant's forehead. Hymir, impressed by this demonstration, told Thor that he could take away the cauldron. This was how Aegir gained a cauldron large enough to brew mead for all the gods.

Another tale of Aegir concerns the banquet he offered to the gods, whom he invited down to his hall at the bottom of the sea. The gods accepted the invitation happily, but regretted the absence from the feast of Balder. Loki, who had used Hodur to murder Balder, was likewise absent but then, to the gods' dismay, appeared. He took pleasure in slandering them all, Sif in particular.

Njord started off as one of the Vanir; he was brought, along with his children Frey and Freya, to Asgard as a hostage at the end of the war between the Aesir and the Vanir. Like Aegir he was a sea god; his special responsibilities were the sea near to the shore and the wind off the sea, as well as fishing and trade. From his hall, Nôatûn, he worked to calm the tempests created far out at sea by Aegir. Despite the fact that their responsibilities differed, Njord in due course took over the Vikings' allegiance from Aegir – aside from anything else, he was seen as a much more beneficent god than Aegir, even though later he was regarded as responsible for storms at sea, as Aegir had been. He was also thought of as being very handsome, a quality that was never widely attributed to Aegir.

The first wife of Njord was Nerthus; some myths equate Nerthus with Frigga, but this cannot have been true because Nerthus was one of the Vanir. Once Njord came to Asgard he had to look around for a new wife. His prayers were answered when, one day, a young giantess called Skadi arrived in Asgard from her home in Thrymheim. Her father had been the giant Thiassi, who had been responsible for kidnapping the goddess Idun; the gods had slain Thiassi after Loki had succeeded in rescuing Idun, and now Skadi wanted some form of reparation. She can be regarded as the Norse equivalent of the Greek Diana: she was associated with hunting and winter. She was also very lovely – but vengeful for the death of her father. The Aesir admitted that she had a valid cause, and offered to give her gold, but she was so furious that she demanded a life in return for the life of her father. The Aesir would have been in trouble had it not been for Loki, who capered and danced (at one point tying his scrotum to a goat) until the giantess's features melted into a smile; the gods then took advantage of her mellowness, pointing to the constellation which they had created from her father's eyes. They added that, rather than kill one of them, she could instead select from among their number a husband – provided that she

would be willing to do so through examination of their naked feet alone. (The chronology of these events in Asgard is given in a different order in different sources.) Perhaps there had been a lot of mead flowing, but she agreed to this condition and looked around for the prettiest pair of feet she could see. And there was a pair of sumptuously formed feet! She assumed they must belong to Balder, the fairest of all the gods, whom she had earlier seen and taken a fancy to. To her horror she discovered that in fact she had selected Njord, and so they had to be married.

In fact, she and Njord had a fine honeymoon in Asgard; all of the Aesir went out of their way to make her feel honoured. Afterwards Njord took her back to Nôatûn – where the trouble started. Although the couple were still fond of each other, Skadi couldn't tolerate the sound of the breakers, the screams of the gulls and the harsh cries of the seals. She told Njord that she would never have another good night's sleep again unless he took her back to Thrymheim. He was so entranced by her that he readily agreed that they could spend nine nights out of every dozen (or nine months of each year – sources differ) there, returning to Nôatûn only for the other three. Unfortunately, he soon came to detest Thrymheim because he was kept awake each night by the din of the frequent avalanches, the whistle of the wind through the pine trees, the crashing of waterfalls, the crackling of the ice and the howling of the wolves.

Njord and Skadi – equated with the summer and the winter – put up with their privations for some time, she spending the three months of summer by the sea and he remaining with her for the other nine months in her home in the mountains. Eventually, though, they agreed that neither of them could put up with the situation much longer, and so they amicably agreed to separate. Long after, Skadi gave birth to Saeming, the first king of Norway; the father was supposed to have been Odin.

BALDER

Balder was the most beautiful of all the gods. He was a son of Odin and Frigga. His twin brother was Hoder but, while Balder, the god of light, was radiantly handsome, poor Hoder, the god of darkness, was blind and gloomy. Nevertheless, the two brothers were deeply devoted to each other, living together in Balder's hall, Breid-ablik, along with Balder's wife Nanna.

Balder had runes carved on his tongue – indeed, he could read all runes. He was also a master of herbal medicine, and he could see the future – except, that is, for the truth about his own fate. As he walked Asgard, loved by mortals and gods alike, he talked of his dreams, which were always of the best. But then his demeanour began to change: he walked slumpedly and defeatedly, and the light vanished from his eyes. When the gods asked why this was he explained that his dreams had now become nightmares bearing with them a presentiment of some terrible fate awaiting him. Balder's mother and father took his fears seriously, and Frigga determined to do something to ensure her son's safety. She accordingly elicited from every object in the world – animals, plants, stones, ores, everything – a promise that they would not harm Balder. The only thing whose promise was not given was the mistletoe but, as the goddess's minions pointed out, this plant was too soft, young and puny to do the great Balder any serious harm.

The gods then, on several occasions, had fun in Gladsheim by testing Balder's new-found invulnerability. They threw rocks at him, fired arrows at him, struck at him with axes and swords – nothing had any effect, and there was much hilarity. One god, though, was not so pleased. This was Loki, who for long had been jealous of Balder's popularity. He schemed the radiant god's downfall. Knowing that

Frigga had given Balder his apparently complete invulnerability, he nevertheless suspected that there might be a loophole. He therefore changed himself into the form of an old woman and came to Frigga where she sat spinning in her hall. It didn't take him long to discover from the goddess that the mistletoe had failed to be enlisted to her cause.

Loki swiftly left her and went to find a bunch of mistletoe. He stripped away most of the berries and branches to leave one that was long and straight; this he sharpened at one end. He then went to the place where the gods were enjoying themselves throwing objects harmlessly at Balder. Loki's eyes fastened on Hoder, who was doing his

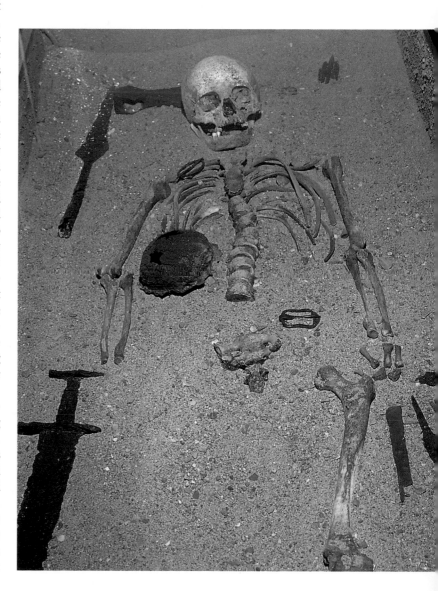

BELOW *To be granted a funeral pyre was a great honour among the Vikings: a lesser honour for a warrior was to be buried alongside his weaponry. Here we see a reconstruction of a grave believed to date from about the tenth century.*

13

best to join in the fun – but with little success, because of his blindness. He went up to Hoder and offered to help him by guiding his hand if he wanted to throw an object – like this sharpened stick that Loki just happened to have with him. Like a fool Hoder agreed to this plan, threw the dart of mistletoe and killed his brother.

Earlier, Odin, worried like Frigga about Balder's future, had travelled to Hel to consult a prophetess. The prophetess had been interred in the grim otherland for many long years, and was unwilling to stir herself. However, Odin – pretending to be a mortal called Vegtam – used runes and magic spells to force her to answer his questions. He pointed around them to where the denizens of Hel were preparing a feast, and asked who the feast was to be in honour of; she responded that it was being readied to welcome Balder, who would soon be slain by his brother Hoder. Odin was grief-stricken, but found the time to press the prophetess into telling him who would avenge Balder's death. She told him that this would be the task of Vali, a god who would be born to Odin and the earth-goddess Rind. Odin then asked the prophetess a further question: would anyone refuse to weep at Balder's death? She immediately guessed that the person speaking to her had foreknowledge of the future and must therefore be Odin, so she refused to answer this last question and descended once more to her grave. Greatly saddened, Odin returned to Asgard, where he was reassured to discover that Frigga – or so she thought – had extracted the promise of all things not to harm Balder.

When the dart of mistletoe killed Balder the gods were horrified. They could see all too well who had been guilty of the crime – Loki – but at the same time their cruel code dictated that it was Hoder who should die to avenge his brother's death. Nevertheless, it was taboo to shed blood in Gladsheim, and so there was nothing they could immediately do. Frigga, however, was less concerned with

vengeance than with the possibility that Balder might – just possibly – be restored to life. She asked the assembled company if there were anyone there who might risk great peril and travel to Hel to ask the goddess of death if there was any way that she might be bribed into releasing Balder back to the land of the living. There was an embarrassingly long silence at this, because the journey to Hel was by no means a pleasant one, but, eventually, when Frigga promised that the brave volunteer would be considered by herself and Odin to be the dearest of all the Aesir, Hermod stepped forward to say that he would perform the task. Soon he was on his way, Odin having lent him his eight-footed horse Sleipnir for the journey.

Once Hermod had departed, it was the duty of the gods to create Balder's funeral pyre, for which they used his ship, Ringhorn, and vast quantities of wood cut from a nearby forest. The gods each added to the pyre their most treasured possessions. In Odin's case this was his ring called Draupnir. As he added it to the pyre he also whispered some words into the dead Balder's ear, but none of the other gods were near enough to hear what those words were.

The preparation of Balder's pyre was too much for the god's wife, Nanna. She collapsed and died, and so was put on Ringhorn beside her husband, to share his fiery fate.

Unfortunately, the gods had loaded Ringhorn so enthusiastically with precious objects that they found themselves incapable of launching the ship. Luckily the mountain giants, who had been watching the whole proceedings, stepped in to offer help. They told the gods that one of their number, a giantess called Hyrrokin, was so strong that she would be able to shove the ship from shore unaided. When the giantess was summoned, she arrived riding an enormous wolf, the pacification of which took the company some while. The Hyrrokin put her shoulder to Ringhorn and with a single heave managed to launch it: the rollers down

RIGHT Hermod, his initial plea to Hel having failed, bids farewell to Balder and Nanna. At this stage Hermod was optimistic, because he believed that all the world would fulfil Hel's condition for releasing the beautiful god by weeping for him. A nineteenth-century book illustration.

which it ran caught fire from the friction and all the worlds shook from the force of her effort. The gods staggered and Thor, for one, was so incensed by the perceived insult that he prepared to assault the giantess with his hammer; luckily the other Aesir pointed out that she had been helping them, and his anger diminished. But soon afterwards a dwarf called Lit got in Thor's way and the god responded by kicking him, still alive, to perish in the flames of the pyre.

Meanwhile Hermod was on his way to Hel, in Niflheim. Finally he crossed the bridge over the river Giöll to reach the dreaded realm, and there he was stopped by the hideous guard called Modgud. She told him that his clattering across the bridge had made more noise than a whole army of the dead who had ridden over it the day before: it seemed pretty clear to her that he was alive, and she demanded to know who he was and why he had come here. He answered her honestly, and she told him that Balder and Nanna had already arrived; she gave him directions to the gates of Hel itself. These seemed impassable at first, but Hermod spurred Sleipnir into a colossal leap, which whisked both of them safely into Hel.

BELOW A Viking sword with a silver and gold hilt found at Dybäck, Skåne. This sword may have been either made in England (the metalwork is typical of that being produced at the time at Winchester) or made in Scandinavia but strongly influenced by the English style.

When he came to Hel's banquet hall, Eljudnir, Hermod found Balder and Nanna. Balder sadly told him that his quest had been at least partly in vain: he was doomed to remain in this place until Ragnarok. However, there was a chance that Hermod could at least take Nanna back to Asgard. But the goddess refused, saying that she preferred to remain with her husband, come what may. Hermod then spoke with the goddess Hel, telling her that all over the nine worlds people were grieving the death of Balder; in this context, he argued, would it not be just to release the god? She thought about this for a time, and then said that she doubted that the grief was quite as universal as Hermod claimed. However, if everything everywhere, living or dead, could prove its sorrow by weeping for the death of Balder she would be prepared to let him and Nanna go. Mind you, should a single person, animal, plant or object refuse to weep, she would hold onto Balder until the end of time. This particular stricture did not much concern Hermod, who knew – or so he thought – that everything and everyone mourned Balder, and so he was happy as he made his way back to Asgard.

Frigga and the other gods sent messengers to every part of the nine worlds to inform all things of what must be done to save Balder. Soon the weeping was universal – even the vilest things of the worlds were sobbing for the loss of the light-god. There was only one dissident, a giantess called Thok. When the messengers told her what she should do she simply mocked them, saying that she'd never much cared for Balder during his life and saw no reason why Hel should not hold onto him forever. Gloomily the messengers returned to Asgard, where at once the gods realized that the news was not good. Soon they guessed that Thok had in fact been Loki in disguise.

Even though Loki had now twice, in effect, murdered Balder, it still seemed to the gods important that Balder's death be avenged by the death of Hoder. Odin therefore paid suit to Rind, a goddess of the frozen earth. She, however, was less than flattered by his attentions, perhaps feeling that it was rather insulting to her that he should merely wish to use her as breeding stock to produce Vali, the avenger of the prophecy. In the end she consented, however, and the eventual result was a baby boy who grew so rapidly from the moment of his birth that on the very first night of his life Vali came to Asgard and slew Hoder with an arrow.

FREY

Frey was one of the Vanir who came to Asgard as a hostage at the end of the struggle between the Vanir and the Aesir; he was the son of Njord and the twin brother of Freya, whom at one point he also married. He was a fertility god and the god of summer, and the cult associated with him seems to have been pretty unpleasant, involving such practices as human sacrifice. His name is often given as Freyr. He was connected with the image of the boar because of his own magical boar Gullinbursti (made by the dwarfs Sindri and Brock at Loki's request); this creature had shining bristles that lit up the world as it flew through the air. Frey also owned the ship Skidbladnir (fashioned by the dwarf Dvalin, again at Loki's request), which could fly through the air and, although large enough to carry all the gods, their horses and their equipment, could, when not in use, be folded up and put in a pocket. Another useful possession was his sword, which under its own motivation would start slaying his enemies as soon as it was drawn from its sheath. His horse was called Blodughofi. His hall was in Alfheim, the realm of the light elves.

Frey is regarded as one of the three major Norse gods – the other two being, of course, Odin and Thor – yet there are surprisingly few tales about him. The most important concerns his love for a frost giantess, Gerda, the daughter of Gymir and Angrboda. Frey first caught sight of her when he was trespassing on Hlidskialf, Odin's great throne from where everything in the nine worlds was visible. Gerda was a figure of pulsating light (she is often associated with the Aurora Borealis, or Northern Lights), and Frey was instantly stricken with lust for her. For ages afterwards he pined, until Njord, worried for his son's welfare, decided to do something about it. Njord summoned his best servant, Skirnir, and told him to find out what was the matter.

Skirnir quizzed Frey and eventually got the truth out of him. The god realized only too well that the union he wanted to seek with Gerda would be unconscionable to gods and mortals alike, yet still he craved her. So he asked Skirnir to go to Gerda and attempt to woo her; the servant agreed on condition that Frey lend him his sword and his horse. He took with him also eleven of the golden apples of eternal youth as well as Odin's magic ring Draupnir.

Blodughofi bore Skirnir swiftly to Jotunheim, where he found that Gymir's hall was surrounded by curtains of coruscating flame; the servant merely spurred the horse to greater speed, and the two of them shot through the fire. They found that the hall was guarded by huge, horrific hounds, who set up such a howling that Gerda was alerted to their arrival.

BELOW Twelfth-century tapestry from Skog Church, Hålsingland, Sweden, showing the battle between Scandinavian paganism (on the left) and the insurgent Christianity (on the right). The three figures on the left are believed to represent the gods Odin, Thor and Frey.

She realized at once that the visitor had been sent by Frey, who had slain her brother Beli in a brawl, but politely asked him in for a horn of mead before sending him on his way. He, however, had other plans, and immediately began to urge Frey's suit – to which she responded forthrightly. Skirnir then tried to bribe her with the apples and with Draupnir, to which she replied in both cases with equal frankness. (The business with the apples, by the way, suggests a link between Gerda and the goddess Idun. It's possible that the two characters were originally one and the same.)

Skirnir abandoned the subtle approach and told her that he would chop her head off if she did not agree to obey Frey's summons. This time she told him that she wasn't scared by his threats and that her father, on getting home, would take great pleasure in taking Skirnir apart. The servant finally used his deadliest threat. Carved on his staff were runes, and he used the magical power of these to lay on her a curse so vile that she was terrified into acquiescence. Refuse and, forever afterwards, he told her, she would be devoured by lust yet remain celibate; be consumed by hunger yet find that all food tasted brackish to her; be confined by Hel's gates and forced to watch that miserable prospect, all the while knowing that she was becoming a repulsive hag. The only way to avoid this miserable fate was to accede to Frey's demands.

This she agreed to do, but said that she would not meet the god for nine nights yet. Frey somehow managed to live through this interminable time and finally the two married. Despite the shocking way in which she had been treated – the whole business, because of the threats, was essentially rape – she came to love him, bearing his child Fiolnir.

A story of the cult of Frey is worth repeating, even though probably quite apocryphal. It was the practice to carry around a carved image of the god on a cart, accompanied by a priestess, so that the faithful could make offerings

and sacrifices to it and therefore ensure good harvests and fertile marriages. It is said that in the 11th century a Norwegian called Gunnar Helming found himself, for some reason, the only person near the cart – apart from the god's lovely young priestess. Helming suddenly had a Good Idea. Thereafter the people visited by the cart were astonished to discover that the wooden figure of the god had miraculously transformed itself into an apparently living young man. The god's enduring characteristic of fertility was in due course evidenced by the changing shape of the priestess. Moreover, this incarnation of the god was willing to walk among mortals and share their food and drink, so they were only too pleased to comply when he suggested that precious gems and coins might make more fitting tributes to him than their previous somewhat tedious offerings and sacrifices. Eventually the Norwegian king, Olaf Tryggvason, heard about this 'miracle', and soon afterwards the god's image became wooden once more.

*ABOVE A bronze
statuette from Lunda,
Sweden, of Frey. His
role as a fertility god is
extremely obvious.*

FREYA

To call Freya a fertility goddess is to euphemize: she was the goddess of sex. Daughter of Njord and twin sister of Frey, she was one of the three Vanir who came to Asgard as hostages at the end of the war between the Vanir and the Aesir; there is some confusion between her and Frigga. The Aesir were so enchanted by her beauty that they granted to her the realm of Folkvang and the hall Sessrymnir; this latter was so well built that it was regarded as impregnable unless the doors were opened by Freya herself. Her chariot was pulled either by her boar Hildisvini or by a number of cats. She owned a falcon coat which she could use to fly around the world in the guise of that bird. Horses were involved with her cult, for reasons, it appears, of orgiastic sex. Besides her role in terms of sex and beauty she had a somewhat grimmer aspect, because she often led parties of Valkyries down to fetch the dead from battlefields, bringing them back to her hall so that they could enjoy all the benefits of the afterlife.

Her first husband was called Od (or Odur), but he deserted her, and thereafter she wept golden tears of grief at all opportunities – such as there were, for her life thereafter was one of unbridled promiscuity. Counting her various conquests is a fraught matter, but we can list her brother Frey (it's possible that the two of them were originally a single god, and that the tale of their sexual relations represents an explanation of the way that, by the time the Eddas were being written, they had become two), Odin and other gods, a man called Ottar, not to mention four very important dwarfs – see below. When, at his *flyting*, Loki cast certain doubts upon her virtue, it is hard not to agree with his accusations. The gods were not alone in looking on her with a merry grin: the giant Hrungnir, during his bet with Odin, admitted that, while he'd prefer Sif, he'd be quite happy to make do with Freya. She did have her standards, though: she refused to sleep with Hrungnir and likewise with the giant Thrym, even though in the case of the latter she was encouraged to do so by Loki and Thor.

Thrym had stolen Thor's hammer, which was bad news for the gods of Asgard. Loki borrowed Freya's falcon skin and flew over the world to try to ascertain who the thief might be; at last he discovered that the culprit was this rather unprepossessing giant, who said that he had buried Miölnir many miles beneath the surface of the Earth and would not surrender it until Freya had been delivered up to him as his bride. Loki thought this was a fair exchange and so, on his return to Asgard, he proposed it to Freya, seconded by Thor. Freya's fury was spectacular to behold, so the gods had to try another tack.

RIGHT *Arthur Rackham's vision of the female sex goddess Freya.*

Heimdall came up with a possible solution. He pointed out that the problem was really Thor's and Loki's, and that therefore they should have the responsibility for solving it. He suggested that Thor should dress in Freya's clothing and pretend to be her; Loki should likewise dress in female garb and act as 'Freya's' handmaiden. This the two gods rather reluctantly did, and then they journeyed in a goat-drawn chariot back to Thrym's hall.

The giant – presumably myopic – took the gods to be the beautiful women they pretended they were, and welcomed them to a wedding banquet attended by many other giants and giantesses. He was a little disconcerted when 'Freya', at dinner, demolished an ox, eight large salmon, two barrels of mead and all the sweet dishes set out, but Loki explained that this feat had come about simply because 'Freya' had been pining for Thrym for days, and hadn't been able to eat a thing. Next Thrym tried to steal a kiss from 'Freya' but was rocked backwards on his feet by the glare he received from his putative bride. Not to worry, explained Loki: that was just a burning look of passion. The giant's sister asked about the dowry but was ignored: Thrym was convinced that a night of mad ecstasy awaited him. He called for the hammer and commanded that it be placed between 'Freya's' knees as a symbol of their marriage. This was a foolish mistake, because Thor proceeded to use Miölnir to slaughter not only Thrym but also every other giant and giantess on the premises.

Freya's exploits with the four dwarfs involved her more directly. She was exploring the world one night when she came across the smithy of four dwarfs called the Brisings, or Brosings. They were in the process of making an ornament (the Brisingamen, generally assumed to have been a necklace) of such exquisite beauty that Freya could hardly believe her eyes: gems and polished metals mingled and glimmered so that it seemed almost to be liquid flame. There was nothing that the goddess would not do to possess that treasure: when the dwarfs declared that she could have it only if she spent a night of lust with each of them in turn she readily assented.

What she hadn't realized was that Loki had seen her leaving Asgard and had followed her. The wizard of lies rushed to tell Odin of her prostitution, and the king of the Aesir was furious – he longed for Freya himself, so to discover that she was disporting herself with four dwarfs hurt him grievously. At the same time, though, the bulk of his wrath was reserved for Loki, the malicious messenger bearing bad news. He told Loki that he was to steal the Brisingamen from Freya: otherwise there would be terrible punishments in store. Loki pointed out that her hall Sessrymnir could be entered only with Freya's permission, and that the command was therefore an unfair one, but Odin's only response was to become even more threatening, so Loki decided that he would do his best.

The wizard of lies had the advantage that he could change his shape at will. It took him a long time before he discovered a tiny aperture through which he could squirm his way into Sessrymnir, but in the end he managed it. There he saw the lovely form of Freya sprawled on her bed but, alas, in such a position that he was unable to reach the clasp of the Brisingamen. He fidgeted and fumbled for a while and then turned himself into a flea; lighting on Freya's breast he bit her, so that she turned over in her sleep, exposing the clasp. Loki swiftly returned to his own form and let himself out of Sessrymnir, taking the Brisingamen.

What happened next is a matter of debate. According to some versions, the god Heimdall – who could hear even grass growing – heard Loki as he was perpetrating the theft and pursued him. The two waged a battle involving considerable shape-shifting until Loki was finally persuaded that, if he valued his life, he should return the Brisingamen to Freya. An alternative is that Loki, as instructed, took the necklace to Odin, who accepted it. When, next morning, Freya discovered the loss of her treasure, she realized that the only possible culprit had to be Loki, and so she went straight to Odin to complain, saying that if he had had anything to do with the theft he was … well, the women of the Norse myths could, as ever, be blunt. His response was not unreasonable: she was calling him a degenerate, yet had she not debased herself by whoring to the dwarfs in order to obtain the Brisingamen? He therefore charged her that, by way of punishment, she should in future adopt as part of her responsibilities the spreading of warfare and misery – otherwise he would keep the Brisingamen forever. Freya was ashamed, but agreed to the bargain: she needed the necklace almost more than she needed her life itself.

Freya, as noted, was no paragon of virtue. It might have been expected that she should have been reviled for her sexuality – especially in a primitive society, where women are commonly expected to be both chaste and willing. Yet she was one of the most important and respected members of the Norse pantheon. Possibly the Vikings recognized a sexual equality – a *fairness* in their attitudes towards the behaviour of the two different sexes – that might well be adopted by many of the 'developed' societies of today.

FRIGGA

Second wife of Odin and mother of Balder, Frigga was the most important goddess in the Norse pantheon. Because of her connection with fertility, there was obviously a marked overlap between her responsibilities and those of Frey and Freya. It seems likely that all three initially had the same identity before Frigga was separated from Frey/Freya and then these two likewise became divided from each other. However, the chronology of all this is hard to establish: in some branches of Teutonic myth Frigga and Freya are regarded as identical – both, for example, have falcon skins that they can wear to fly around the nine worlds – yet Frey has his own personality. However, Frigga seems always to have been a much gentler fertility goddess than Freya: where the latter represented rampant sex and was associated with a good deal of violence, Frigga was much more associated with that aspect of fertility related to placid domesticity, conjugal happiness and maternity – she was often represented with a bunch of keys at her waist, the symbol of the good housewife. It should not be assumed, however, that she was a consistently obedient spouse: the myths suggest that, early on, she enjoyed adultery with Odin's brothers Ve and Vili and later, often enough, she would work to trick Odin in order to advance the cause of someone she preferred. Frigga's hall was called Fensalir, and she spent much of her time sitting there spinning golden thread or brightly coloured clouds.

Her parentage is something of a conundrum. According to some versions she was the daughter of Odin and the very early goddess Jörd; alternatively she was Jörd's sister, both of them being daughters of the giantess Fiorgyn. Either way, she became Odin's wife and, alone among all the other deities, was permitted to sit upon Hlidskialf, his great throne from which one could see everything that was going on in all the worlds. In addition to this shared omniscience she had also the ability to foretell the future, but she was ever loth to tell what she saw there. She was, perhaps, a little too fond of glorious attire for her own good, but that seems to have been her only notable sin.

It was a sin that could get her into trouble, though, as we discover from one tale (which bears strong resemblances to the story of Freya and the Brisingamen). Odin had had erected a statue of himself and, never modest, had placed a piece of gold inside it. Frigga was keen to have made for her by the dwarfs a magnificent necklace,

LEFT *Nineteenth-century book illustration showing Frigga with some of her handmaidens. These handmaidens were goddesses in their own right.*

and so she stole the piece of gold for the dwarfs to use. The product of their labours was of amazing beauty – so much so that Odin fell even further in love with her than he had been before. However, he was less than amused when, a little later, he discovered that it had been made from gold stolen from his statue. He immediately summoned the dwarfs and demanded that they tell him who was the thief, but they refused to betray the secret. Odin next composed runes so that the statue would be given the power of speech: it was to be placed high on a gate, and sooner or later would tell the truth of the theft to the world.

Frigga was terrified to hear of all this. She summoned her attendant Fulla and instructed the hapless servant to find some way of avoiding Odin's discovery of the crime and his subsequent wrath. Fulla soon returned in the company of a revoltingly ugly dwarf, who promised that he would stop the statue from speaking if Frigga would sleep with him. Hardly sooner said than done, and the following morning the dwarf went to the gate, magically made the guards fall into a deep sleep and shattered the statue, so that Odin would never be able to reconstitute it and discover the truth it was willing to tell.

23

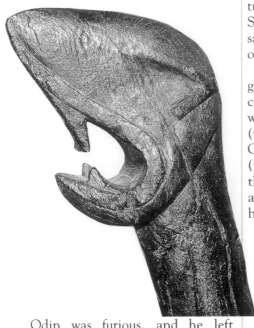

RIGHT *A superb animal head, probably from the bow of a Viking longship, discovered during recent dredging of the River Scheldt, Belgium.*

waited until he was fast asleep and then turned his bed around the other way. Sure enough, when Odin awoke he saw the Winilers and, a man of honour, he gave them the victory.

Frigga is identified with many other goddesses in various mythologies. A complete list would be impossible: here we can note Bertha, Brechta, Eástre (from which the term 'Easter' comes), Gode, Hlodin, Holda, Horn, Nerthus (who also features in the Norse pantheon), Ostara and Wode. As the archetypal Earthmother, of course, she has parallels in almost all mythologies.

HEIMDALL

Odin was furious, and he left Asgard and his favourite wife for seven long months. During this time, perhaps assuming that Odin had abdicated his throne, Ve and Vili took power – and also, according to some sources, enjoyed Frigga's sexual favours. However, they did not have the powers of Odin, and so both Asgard and Midgard were mightily relieved when the great god returned to reassume his throne.

Frigga and Odin often walked Midgard together – although she was a much less frequent traveller than he was. A major legend of one of these ventures concerns Agnar and Geirrod; here Frigga successfully tricked her husband. Another tale of her wiles concerns a war between the Vandals and the Winilers – a war that the heavenly couple had watched with interest from Hlidskialf. Odin was very much on the side of the Vandals, whereas Frigga much preferred the Winilers. One night Frigga asked Odin which of the two sides would win the war on the morrow and he, evasively, said that it would be whichever he first saw. His stratagem was that, because of the direction in which his couch was turned, the first army to meet his gaze would necessarily be that of the Vandals. But he hadn't reckoned with Frigga's cunning. She simply

Heimdall is a somewhat enigmatic member of the Norse pantheon, in that it is unclear whether he was a member of the Aesir or of the Vanir. The identity of his father is uncertain (it was probably Odin), but his mothers were nine giantesses called the Wave Maidens, themselves daughters of Aegir, who together managed to produce this single son. A gynaecological mystery. Heimdall, the White God, the Golden-Toothed, had a trumpet called the Giallar-horn whose tone could be heard throughout the nine worlds; he will use it to announce the onset of Ragnarok. This instrument symbolized the crescent Moon; the god sometimes hung it on one of Yggdrasil's branches and other times put it in Mimir's well, where it lay alongside Odin's lost eye, a symbol of the full Moon. His hall in Asgard was called Himinbiorg and his horse Gulltop (Gold-tuft). He was regarded as the epitome of beauty, brightness, wisdom and goodness.

Heimdall had the task of guarding the rainbow bridge Bifrost to stop the giants attempting to invade Asgard. In order to make this job easier, the gods gave him incredibly acute senses – a sparrow falling would have sounded like a thunderclap to him, because he could hear the wool growing on a sheep's back – and the ability to require little or no sleep. In addition, along with Bragi, he welcomed heroes to Valhalla.

Clearly Heimdall shared many of the attributes of Balder. He also had, like Odin, a habit of wandering among mortals and siring children. In so doing, he started off the lines of the three different classes of human beings. The three legends involved are very much the same. In the first of them, Heimdall – pretending to be a mortal called Riger or Rig – visited a rickety old hut where a husband and wife called Ai (Great Grandfather) and Edda (Great Grandmother) lived. They invited him in for a fairly un-palatable meal, and he ended up stay-ing with them for three nights. Each night he slept between the couple on their bed, and presumably Ai was a sound sleeper because, nine months later, Edda gave birth to Heimdall's son Thrall. The boy was not the most physically prepossessing of fellows, but he was mightily strong and was willing to work from dawn until dusk. He mar-ried a woman called Thir who was like-wise a willing worker and soon they gave birth to a plentiful brood of child-ren, who were the first members of the class of serfs.

Meanwhile Heimdall had been repeating exactly the same act else-where. Afi (Grandfather) and Amma (Grandmother) welcomed him for three nights in similar circumstances, although the food was somewhat better and certainly there was plenty of it. Nine months later a boy called Karl appeared; he proved to be an excellent farmer and, with his wife Snor, who was prudent and, it seems, notable for the ampleness of her bosom. Their children became the first of the peasant class.

The food was much better when Heimdall stayed three nights with Fadir (Father) and Modir (Mother); the accompanying wines were first-class, too. Perhaps for these reasons, the result of the clandestine mating, Jarl, was delicate, handsome and refined.

He soon learned to use the runes and to be very good at killing people; he and his aristocratic wife Erna became the ancestors of the ruling and warrior classes. The youngest of their children was a boy called Konur or Kon, who was if anything even more remarkable than his father. He had the strength of eight men and could speak with the birds, douse fires, still the sea, blunten blades and ease troubled hearts. Un-fortunately, because of the fragmented nature of the surviving manuscripts we know little more about Konur except

BELOW Part of a carved cross slab found at Jurby, Isle of Man, Britain, depicting Heimdall blowing his horn to summon the gods to Ragnarok.

that he, or one of his descendants, became the first king of Denmark.

Heimdall's wisdom was useful to the Aesir. When the giant Thrym demanded to have Freya as his bride if he were to return Thor's hammer, it was Heimdall who proposed the plan whereby Thor and Loki travelled in female garb to Thrym's hall. In fact, he seems to have been a champion of Freya's somewhat frail virtue, because there are fragments of another myth in which he wrestled with Loki for the return to her of the Brisingamen. The two gods indulged in a battle of shape-changing (a version of which, fought between Merlin and Madam

25

Mim, appeared in the 1963 Disney movie *The Sword in the Stone*). Loki became a flame and Heimdall a cloud to rain on him; Loki became a polar bear and prepared to swallow the water but Heimdall became another bear and attacked him; both of them became seals and struggled in the water, with Heimdall being the eventual winner. As he will be in the very last resort: Loki, bound until Ragnarok, will eventually be slain by Heimdall, although the White God will lose his own life at the same time.

BELOW Detail of an eighth-century stela found in Gotland, Sweden, showing a Scandinavian warrior on horseback.

IDUN

Idun, the wife of Bragi, was the goddess of Spring and the guardian of the gods' eternal youth. This youthfulness was incorporated in the form of golden apples, which she kept in a magic basket; no matter how many apples she removed from the basket to give to the gods during their feasting there was always still the same number left. Idun reserved her apples exclusively for the gods, who therefore remained young and vigorous while all other beings grew old and died. Naturally the apples were coveted by the dwarfs and giants, and this fact led to Idun's major adventure.

Odin, Hoenir and Loki were one day wandering in the world when they became hungry. Spotting a nearby herd of cattle they promptly killed one of the beasts, made a fire and roasted it. However, when in due course they kicked away the embers of the fire and sat down to eat they discovered that the ox was hardly cooked at all. They tried again, but still without success. At that moment a huge eagle spoke to them, saying that its magic had been stopping the flames from cooking the flesh, and offering the three Aesir a deal: the eagle would remove the spell so that the gods could cook their dinner, but they were to give the bird as much to eat as it wanted. This seemed fair enough to the Aesir, and the bargain was struck.

They hadn't reckoned on the eagle's appetite. It took the shoulder joints and the rump of the ox for its own portion, leaving the gods with not very much. This drove Loki into a fury, and he picked up a branch and plunged it into the bird's back. The eagle dropped the meat and flew off, still impaled by the branch, which Loki now found his hands were stuck to. Low over the ground they flew, so that Loki was bumped and dragged along, being bruised and battered and cut and torn until he was in agony. He screamed for mercy, and finally the bird agreed that it would release him if he would promise to do something for it: lead Idun out from the safety of Asgard so that she could be captured. Loki rapidly agreed to do this and the eagle – who was in fact a giant called Thiassi in disguise – let him go.

Some while later Loki went to Idun and told her that he had discovered a grove where apples grew that were in every respect like her magic ones. Credulously she accepted his offer to lead her to this place. However, as soon as they were out of Asgard he deserted her. Thiassi, again in his guise as an eagle, swooped down from the skies and carried the goddess away to his hall, crowing that at last he had captured the gift of eternal youth. He was deeply chagrined to discover that Idun – although she had always seemed such an ineffectual goddess – refused to let him have a single apple.

It was not long before things at Asgard began to go badly wrong. The Aesir, who had initially assumed the Idun had gone away with her minstrel husband Bragi on one of his ramblings, became very worried about her, especially when they started wrinkling with age and losing their reason to senility. Odin summoned the Aesir to a conference, and when they were gathered they discovered that all were present except Loki. Even their aging brains didn't take long to work out that the wizard of lies had been up to some more of his mischief, and their suspicions were confirmed when one of the servants of Heimdall announced that, the last time he'd seen Idun, she'd been going over Bifrost with Loki.

The other gods made it plain to Loki in no uncertain manner that, unless he got them out of this mess – and quickly – his end was not going to be an enjoyable one. He therefore borrowed Freya's falcon-skin and flew off to Thiassi's hall, Thrymheim. Luckily the giant wasn't there. Loki turned Idun into a nut and, clutching her in his claws, flew back towards Asgard.

When Thiassi returned and found the goddess gone he was furious. At once he adopted the form of a huge eagle once more, and set off in hot pursuit of Loki. And so it was that, when the gods looked out from Asgard to watch for Loki's return, they saw not only the falcon but also, in chase, the great black eagle. The Aesir swiftly gathered up a great heap of fuel. As the falcon flopped exhaustedly into Asgard bearing its precious burden, they set light to the fuel so that Thiassi flew straight into a wall of flames. Burnt and stunned, the eagle crumpled to the ground, where it was swiftly despatched by the Aesir. Later, however, mellowed by a feast of apples and feeling young and fresh again, they threw Thiassi's eyes up into the sky to form a constellation, a tribute which they reckoned would placate any vengeful relatives of the dead giant. (They thought wrong. His daughter Skadi came to Asgard to demand recompense. However, she relented and instead ended up marrying Njord.)

Another legend about Idun has largely been lost to us. It seems that one day she accidentally fell into Niflheim where she went into a frozen and horrified coma. Odin sent Bragi and a couple of the other gods down there after her with some skins to warm her, but they were unable to get her to respond. In the end Bragi told the other two to leave them there, and that he would keep his wife company until she was ready to go. What happened next is, sadly, unrecorded.

LOKI

There are far more tales about Loki than about any of the other gods. The reader is referred to the index for reference to those legends involving Loki that are not discussed here.

Loki, the wizard of lies, the god of mischief and deception, is the most fascinating of all the members of the Norse pantheon, not just because of his wiles and cunning but because he shows that rarest of things in a mythological personage, character development. Although never to be trusted, in the early days he helped Odin create the world and then was useful to the other gods on countless occasions. Later his mischief took on a more malevolent nature, as when he chopped off the hair of Sif (q.v.). But he then became actively evil, arranging for the murder of Balder (q.v.) and committing other hideous crimes – as we shall see.

Loki married three times. His first wife was called Glut and she bore him

RIGHT *The western face of Gosforth Cross, Cumbria, Britain, which dates from the tenth century. At the bottom is the chained Loki beneath the serpent; Sigyn, above the serpent, is catching the venom in a cup. Above this scene is Odin, and at the top we see Heimdall being attacked by two dragons.*

the children Einmyria and Eisa; all three names refer to fire and its warmth, since in one of his aspects Loki was the charming god of the fireside, relaxation and leisure. For this reason the peasant classes maintained he was the greatest of all the gods – understandably, because the few moments of leisure they had must have been as precious as gold dust to them. The offspring of his second marriage were less pleasant. This time his wife was a giantess called Angrboda, and their children were Hel, the goddess of death, Jormungand, the World Serpent, and Fenris, the monstrous wolf who came to threaten the very existence of the gods. Loki's third wife was the beautiful Sigyn; their two children were Narvi and Vali (not to be confused with the god called Vali).

As noted, Loki could be very useful to the gods. One such instance occurred when they made a foolish promise. A giant came to Asgard and offered to build a protective wall around it. There was some haggling over his fee, but eventually the gods agreed that he could have the hand of Freya if he could complete the task within a single winter, six months – something they believed to be impossible. Their reasoning was that they could get at least part of the wall built for nothing, saving themselves a deal of hard work. They hadn't reckoned on the giant's horse, a doughty animal that was capable of performing prodigious feats of labour, never ceasing by night or day. As time passed, it began to dawn on the gods that it was very likely that the giant might indeed succeed in his task; then they realized that it was a certainty, and, not wishing to lose Freya, they turned to Loki for help. The last morning of the six months came and there were only a few stones left to be put in place. Then out from Asgard danced a sexy little mare; she whinnied suggestively at the giant's horse and then, with a swish of her tail, danced off into the forest. Suddenly the giant didn't have his equine assistant any longer, and saw that he had no chance of finishing the wall.

He was dejected about having been cheated, and Thor killed him. When the mare returned to Asgard she was the proud mother of a foal, the eight-legged horse Sleipnir, which became Odin's mighty steed.

Another instance of Loki's helpfulness occurred when the giantess Skadi came to Asgard seeking vengeance for the slaying of her father Thiassi. Loki entertained her with lewd knockabout humour until she relented and became the wife of Njord (*q.v.*).

The trickster could also befriend humans. A peasant gambled on a game of chess with the giant Skrymsli: if the giant won his prize was to be the peasant's son, unless the boy could be hidden so well that he could not be found. And, of course, the giant did win. The grief-stricken peasant turned to Odin for help, and the god changed the lad into a tiny grain of wheat. However, Skrymsli immediately saw through this subterfuge, went to the field in which the boy was concealed and mowed the wheat until at last he came to the right grain. Odin snatched it from his hand at the last moment, returned the boy to his parents and then lost interest in the whole matter. Next the peasants turned to Hoenir, who transformed the boy into a tiny down feather which he placed on the breast of a swan. Again the giant saw through the trick, and would have eaten the down feather had not Hoenir puffed it away from his mouth.

Like Odin, this god then lost interest, so the peasants begged Loki to assist them. He turned the boy into a single egg in a fish's roe. Skrymsli managed to see through this ruse as well, and after some inspired angling was able to draw from the sea the very fish in which the boy was hidden. The giant was picking through the roe looking for the correct egg when Loki snatched it from his grasp and ran away with it. He turned the egg back into the boy again, and told him to flee for home but to make sure, as he did so, to pass through the boathouse where Loki, having taken precautions against failure, had rigged up a sharp spike.

The boy did as he was told and ran off, and Skrymsli, chasing him, seriously injured himself.

Loki chopped off one of the giant's legs but almost immediately it began to join back on to Skrymsli's torso. Swiftly the god realized that there was magic at work, so he chopped off Skrymsli's other leg and this time placed flint and steel between the limb and the body, thus rendering the magic inoperative, so that the giant bled to death.

But Loki could be randomly cruel. One day he, Odin and Hoenir were out walking when Loki spotted an otter by a riverbank preparing to eat a salmon. The god threw a stone accurately and killed the animal, claiming its salmon for the trio's meal. However, this was no ordinary otter: it was Otter, one of the sons of the dwarfish king Hreidmar. So began the whole miserable business of Andvari's gold.

As we saw, Loki's children by the giantess Angrboda were Hel, Jormungand and Fenris. The marriage had been unauthorized and so he tried to

29

RIGHT *Thorwald's Cross Slab, at Andreas, Isle of Man, Britain, dating from about the tenth century and showing Odin being attacked by Fenris at Ragnarok.*

keep the children hidden in a cave, but they grew very rapidly and so it wasn't very long before Odin discovered their existence. The father of the gods determined to get rid of them before they grew so large that they threatened all the world. He cast Hel into Niflheim, in which dismal realm she reigned gloomily as the goddess of death. The snake Jormungand he threw into the sea, where it grew so huge that soon it encircled the entire world and was able to swallow its own tail. Odin was rather alarmed that Loki's offspring could grow so prodigiously, and he looked at Fenris with new nervousness. Might it not be a good idea to try to educate the wolf into the ways of gentleness? He brought Fenris to Asgard.

The gods were terrified of the beast – all except Tyr, the god of courage, who was therefore given the task of tending him. Still Fenris continued to grow in both size and ferocity. The gods were unwilling to kill the wolf, which had been brought to Asgard as a guest, so they decided to bind him so securely that he would never be able to threaten them again. They got hold of a strong chain called Laeding and set to work. Fenris just grinned: he was confident in his own strength, so he waited until they had finished and then casually snapped the chain into a million pieces. The gods tried again with an even stronger chain, Droma, but the result was much the same, although this time Fenris had to struggle a little harder and longer.

A servant of Frey's called Skirnir was sent to ask the dwarfs to make a tether so strong that nothing could ever break it. They gave him a slender strand, Gleipnir, made out of the sound of a cat's footfall, the voice of a fish and other such intangibles. The gods told Fenris that surely, after his exploits with the chains, he couldn't be scared of embarking on this new test of his strength, but he had inherited some of his father's wiliness and looked at it suspiciously, eventually agreeing to be tied up in it only if one of the gods would put a hand in

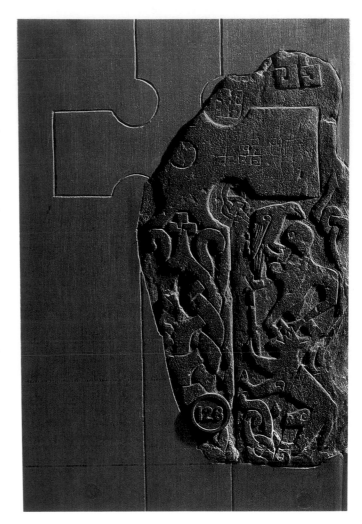

his (Fenris's) mouth as an earnest that no magic was involved. Nobody was willing to do this except Tyr, who lost his hand when the secured Fenris discovered that he had been duped.

The wolf was then placed beneath the ground, but he howled with such abandon that the gods couldn't stand the noise. To silence him the Aesir put a sword vertically in his mouth, with its point in his palate; blood flowed forth to form a great river. And so Fenris will stay until Ragnarok, when Gleipnir will be sundered and he can exact his revenge on the gods. There is an interesting parallel here with Loki's own fate, as we shall see.

Loki's tricks became more and more spiteful. With his lies and his habit of revealing secrets he constantly stirred the gods against each other. One of his worst tricks was the shearing of Sif's (q.v.) magnificent hair. It was as a result of this and his wager with Brock and Sindri that Loki suffered the agonies of having his lips stitched up. The gods' lack of sympathy for – indeed, their merriment over – his torment was probably what turned his petty maliciousness into a vindictive lust to destroy them.

Balder (q.v.), of course, he did destroy, and thereafter he decided that it would be prudent not to show his face in Asgard for a while. The gods were grief-stricken. In order to try to cheer them up a bit, the sea-god Aegir threw a banquet; naturally enough, Loki was not on the guest list. However, he turned up anyway, contributing to the merriment by murdering one of Aegir's servants and insulting all of the gods in the most vitriolic terms, as recorded in a riveting *flyting* ('insult poem'). Their wrath was intensified by the fact that many of the insults were all too true. Freya, for example, he labelled as a whore because she had slept with the entire male pantheon (including her own brother), uncountable dwarfs, and so on; her response was to tell him that he was lying – but for once, of course, he wasn't. The diatribe continued until Thor threatened to hammer him to death, at which he fled.

The gods decided that enough was enough: something had to be done about Loki. They decided to bind him, much as they had his son Fenris. But first, of course, there was the task of finding him.

Loki was all too well aware that the Aesir would try to track him down. Although he lived quietly in a little shack, he knew that Odin's all-seeing eyes would be able to spot him. He therefore determined that, should the gods come to seek him out, he'd jump into a nearby river and take the form of a salmon. Then he began to worry that the other Aesir might catch on to this ruse: a hook he could, as a highly intelligent salmon, avoid with ease – but what if they used a net? Most nets he would have little trouble in breaking, but perhaps they could make one especially strong ... The thought nagged away at him. He reckoned that he was the cleverest of the gods: if *he* couldn't make such a net then none of the others would be able to. In an attempt to set his mind at rest he gathered cord and set to work.

To his alarm he found that it would indeed be possible to make a net capable of catching him. He was halfway through the task when he perceived that Odin, Thor and Kvasir were approaching his shack. In a panic, he threw the half-finished net on the fire to destroy the evidence, ran off and jumped into the river.

The three vengeful gods looked around the empty shack. It seemed that Loki had left no trace of where he had gone to, but then Kvasir, the wisest of all the gods, spotted the stranded ashes of the burnt net. After a little thought, he realized that Loki must have turned himself into a fish, and suggested that the trio quickly weave a net and trawl the river.

The first time they threw the net Loki was able to escape: he put himself between two stones so that the net couldn't reach him. The three gods had an inkling that this might have been his stratagem, and so, next time around, they weighted the net. Loki avoided it by jumping over it against

31

the current, something fish had heretofore never been able to do. However, his leap was seen by the gods, and so they tried again with the weighted net. This time, as Loki jumped over it, Thor was ready and waiting and was able to catch him by the tail.

The three of them dragged him away to bind him – both as punishment for his crimes and to ensure that never again would he plague them. They took him to a deep cavern. Believing that the sins of the fathers should be visited on the children, they induced Loki's son Vali to become a wolf and rip out the throat of his other son, Narvi. From Narvi's corpse they extracted the entrails, and these they used to tie up Loki to three great rocks; as an afterthought they turned the guts into iron, to make doubly sure that Loki would be unable to escape until Ragnarok. Skadi – the giantess whom

Loki had charmed so long ago – decided that his fate hadn't been nearly nasty enough. She fetched a serpent and hung it over Loki's head, so that its venom would drip, second after second, into his face for the rest of eternity – until Ragnarok. Naturally, every drop of venom caused him unspeakable pain. Sigyn, Loki's wife, was not only beautiful but also virtuous and faithful. She could have gone back to Asgard, and enjoyed the life of the gods, but instead she resigned herself to staying beside her husband for all the rest of time, catching the drips in a cup held above his face. She is still there. From time to time, however, the cup becomes filled and she has to empty it. During those moments the venom falls onto Loki's face and he screams in agony.

Come Ragnarok, the gods will regret their cruelty.

BELOW *Made from walrus ivory around 1135–1150 and found on the Isle of Lewis, Scotland, these pieces come from a Viking chess set.*

RIGHT *Nineteenth-century book illustration of Odin's wild hunt; traditionally Odin rode on eight-legged Sleipnir for this, but here we can see that the artist has omitted the extra four legs. Gales were considered to be the physical manifestations of Odin leading his wild hunt across the sky.*

ODIN

Odin is often called Allfather, which is the name of the primordial deity who initiated the Creation; in fact, in many of the legends it is assumed that the two gods are one and the same. This may seem like an inconsistency in the mythology – and probably is – but we should remind ourselves that there is a parallel in Christianity, where Christ is both God and the son of God. A further resemblance to this situation is found in a legend relating how Odin, pierced by a spear, was hanged for nine days and nights from a branch of Yggdrasil as a sacrifice to himself. During this time he learned great wisdoms and invented the runes; he became the patron god of hanged men.

There are many tales in this book about Odin: the reader is referred to the index for most of them. Here we shall look at only a few.

Odin required no food, although he would partake of the gods' heavenly mead. His spear was Gungnir, which always found its mark; in addition, it had the property that any oath sworn upon it could never be broken. He owned the magical golden ring called Draupnir: every ninth night this would shed eight replicas of itself. His steed Sleipnir, a son of Loki (q.v.), had eight legs and could travel at colossal speed all over the nine worlds. His high throne in Asgard was called Hlidskialf, and when seated on it Odin could see everything that happened anywhere; Frigga (q.v.), his second wife, was allowed to sit here also. (His other two wives were Jörd and Rind.) Further information from the worlds was brought to him by his two ravens, Hugin and Munin, who flew from Asgard each morning and returned each evening. He was the master of

LEFT *From the ninth
century, the skull of a
woman sacrificed at a
Viking ship burial at
Ballyteare, Isle of Man,
Britain. It can be seen
that the top of her head
was chopped off.*

two wolves, Freki and Geri, which he personally fed with gobbets of raw meat. He was one-eyed because he had drunk from the well of the wise god Mimir, and had willingly surrendered an eye for the continuing wisdom he received.

He was instrumental in starting the war between the Vanir and the Aesir. A witch called Gullveig – probably one of the Vanir – came to Asgard and explained to Odin and the other Aesir that she was consumed by the lust for gold. The Aesir were revolted by her avariciousness, and determined to put her to death; they tried this three times. The Aesir then gave up their attempts and the witch, now called Heid, was permitted to wander Asgard. (There is a possibility that Heid and Freya were really one and the same.) However, the Vanir were enraged when they heard how she had been treated, and soon it was clear that there must be conflict between the two races of gods. The war began when Odin impatiently threw his great spear at the rallied Vanir.

Odin's halls were Gladsheim, Valaskialf and Valhalla; the last of these is discussed later in this book.

The cult of Odin spread far further eastwards than one might have expected. There is no room here to discuss the matter in detail, but it is worth looking at one aspect. There are mentions in the myths of wives being killed, or killing themselves, at the funerals of their warrior husbands – the death of Nanna at the funeral of Balder (*q.v.*) is one example. This seems to have been a regular habit of the Vikings, because double graves have been found in plenty. The practice seems to have diffused eastward across Europe and Asia, and has obvious connections with the Indian ritual of *suttee*. However, as with so many aspects of cultural archaeology, it is almost impossible to work out the directions in which ideas spread.

Odin was simultaneously a wise, a kind and a cruel god, and as such he may represent human nature – for all of us can be simultaneously wise, kind and cruel.

35

SIF

Not a lot is known about the goddess Sif. She seems to have been a fertility goddess whose prominence had faded by the time the chroniclers were writing their tales. Thor was her second husband; to her first, an anonymous frost giant, she bore a son called Uller. Her sons by Thor were called Magni and Modi.

The reason for guessing that she was connected with fertility is that she had a mane of beautiful golden hair that reached all the way to the ground; this is taken to represent abundant corn. She was extremely proud of her hair, as was Thor, so neither of them were terribly amused when one night as she slept someone came along and cut it all off. When things like that happened in Asgard, the culprit was invariably Loki. Thor responded to the situation with his usual subtlety, and so a few moments later a battered and bloodied Loki discovered that he'd promised that somehow – anyhow – he'd get Sif a new head of hair from somewhere. No, not a wig: it had to be genuine, growing, golden hair.

Such things are not easy to procure, and Loki knew that he had no alternative but to seek aid from the master craftsmen of the nine worlds, the dwarfs of Svartalfaheim. He went to the smithy of a dwarf called Dvalin and persuaded him to make the hair. The dwarf did a miraculous job (literally: the dwarfs could use rune-magic as much as physical skill in their work) and, despite the fact that all Loki offered by way of payment was a string of empty promises, went on to create also Frey's magic ship Skidbladnir and Odin's magic spear Gungnir. Loki was amazed by the magnificence of these gifts and also by the gullibility of the dwarf, who had done so much for so little payment.

He was on his way back to Asgard when a thought struck him. If one dwarf could be so easily duped,

mightn't others be likewise? No sooner thought than tried! Instants later he was showing the three treasures to two dwarfs called Brock and Sindri (in some versions Eitri) and enthusing to them over how, surely, no dwarf could ever hope again to make anything quite as fine – in fact, the god got so carried away that he bet the two dwarfs that, if they could craft anything better, as judged by the gathered Aesir, they could chop off his head! 'All right,' said the dwarfs smugly, and it was at that moment that Loki realized he might have made a mistake.

Sindri told Brock to keep the bellows blowing consistently, without any pause whatsoever, while he himself went off to mutter the appropriate runes. As Brock worked away an insect flew in and landed on his hand, stinging him very painfully, but he didn't miss a beat. When Sindri reappeared they pulled from the forge Gullinbursti, the great magical boar that Frey would use to ride across the sky. The dwarfs set to work making the next artefact. This time while Sindri was out of the smithy chanting the runes the gadfly reappeared and stung Brock on the cheek. Once again, the doughty dwarf managed to keep up the regular pumping of the bellows – although he must have been becoming pretty suspicious about the shape-changer Loki's reputation for honest wagering. And this time the product of the forge was the magical golden ring (or armlet) Draupnir which, every ninth night, would produce eight others identical with itself; in time it was to become the property of Odin.

Loki realized that these two treasures were almost beyond compare and that there was a very good chance that the Aesir might prefer them to the others. This time, as Brock was pumping away, the gadfly stung him on the eyelid, so that blood ran down into the dwarf's eye. Blinded, he took his hand away from the bellows for just a moment to wipe the blood away. The object the two dwarfs then drew from the forge was the mighty hammer Miölnir, which would of course be-

LEFT *Discovered in a tenth-century Swedish Viking grave – Arab coins. Clearly the Viking civilization had contacts far beyond the geographical limits we popularly assume.*

BELOW *At Ragnarok Thor will battle Jormungand, the World Serpent. Also in this nineteenth-century book illustration we can see Odin fighting Fenris and Frey struggling with Surt. The figure on the right is probably Tyr. In the background is Bifrost.*

come the property of Thor. It was perfect in every respect except for the fact that its handle was perhaps just a trifle too short.

Loki and the dwarfs went to Asgard with all six of these wonderful gifts. The god was not particularly worried, because of the imperfection of Miölnir. The gifts were handed out to their various recipients, and the Aesir marvelled at all of them. Sif's golden hair, everyone agreed, was if anything more splendid than her previous mane had been. However, they pointed out that Miölnir, wielded by Thor, was the most valuable of all the gifts because it could guard them from the predations of the giants.

The gods laughed as Loki tried to bargain his way out of this one. They were still laughing when he fled from the hall. Brock begged Thor, on the honour of the Aesir, to bring the wizard of lies back so that the wager could be completed, and the huge god recognized the force of this argument. He fetched Loki and placed him in front of the others, and all waited for the execution. However, Loki had been thinking further. His head, it was true, was forfeit to Brock and Sindri, but not his neck: if the dwarfs could find some way of decapitating him without harming his neck then he would be the last to stop them.

The Aesir and the dwarfs realized that, alas, Loki had a point here (shades of *The Merchant of Venice*). But the reason the dwarfs had wanted Loki's head was to stop his mischievous lying. Brock therefore said that he would be content to sew up Loki's lips, and this he did with Sindri's magic awl. The god's agony was excruciating, and he ran from the place screaming as he tore away the thongs. The Aesir laughed all the more merrily at his discomfiture, which was perhaps unwise of them, because thereafter Loki became ever more malicious.

THOR

The god of thunder was among the most important three in the Norse pantheon, the others being Odin (obviously) and Loki. He was responsible for the weather and crops, as well as for sea-voyages that might be affected by the weather. Interestingly, the cracking of the sky during thunderstorms was not regarded with dread by the Norse: instead, they regarded it as a sign that Thor was carrying out his responsibilities, which were, essentially, the slaughter of giants. We can wonder if, perhaps, the Scandinavians equated the crashing of thunder with the equally loud sounds of sintering glaciers, because the frost giants were of course connected with the glaciers that were so much a feature of the northern part of the Viking terrain.

As sophisticated as he was gentle, Thor was red-bearded, gluttonous and loud-voiced: his standard way of dealing with any problem was to kill anyone foolish enough to be nearby. Perhaps for this reason he has been enduringly loved. His most significant manifestation in popular culture during this century being the long-running series of his adventures published in the comics. His invincible hammer was Miölnir and his wife was the beautiful goddess Sif; it is hard to work out which of the two he loved the more, but we can guess it was the hammer. Thor, because of his violent encounter with the giant Hrungnir, will spend all of the rest of time until Ragnarok with a stone implanted in his head.

The tales of Thor's adventures can be found on many pages of this book: the reader is referred to the index. Here are a few not-covered elsewhere. The story of Thor and Hrungnir and how the former got a lump of stone in his head clearly demonstrates Thor's approach to things.

It all started when Odin was out on one of his rambles around the world. Astride his eight-legged steed

RIGHT *'Thor' is still very popular as a placename and personal name in Iceland and the Faeroe Islands; when linked to a placename it seems to indicate local worship of the god. This is Torshavn ('Thor's Harbour') in the Faeroes.*

Sleipnir, the father of the gods came to the hall of the giant Hrungnir, generally known to be the strongest of all the giants. It was only moments later that Odin and Hrungnir agreed a wager: Sleipnir versus the giant's horse, Gullfaxi (Golden-mane) – the prize, should Odin lose, being his own head.

Soon the two riders were spurring their steeds into action, and soon after that Odin, realizing that the giant's horse might indeed be the swifter of the two, was galloping very speedily indeed towards Asgard, where he knew Hrungnir could not follow. For his part the giant didn't notice what direction they were taking until he found himself just outside Valhalla – not the best of discoveries, for it was likely to mean that he'd lost his life. The giant was understandably furious about this deception but prepared to meet his doom; luckily the Aesir recognized that he had been rather ill done-by and, instead of killing him, invited him in for a meal.

39

Mead was swallowed in pints, then quarts, and then gallons; the giant followed this act by consuming whole oceans of mead. Hrungnir began to wax large on his ambition to destroy Asgard and all the gods and goddesses dwelling there, with the exception of Freya and Sif, whom he respected for something other than their minds. This caused the sort of frigid silence most of us have experienced at mortal dinner parties.

And it was at this stage that Thor came back from one of his journeys. He was incensed to discover that Hrungnir was there in the first place, and even more so that the giant was regarding his (Thor's) wife, Sif, with a certain degree of mental impropriety. The god proposed to resolve this little argument by hammering the giant's head down between his shoulderblades. The other Aesir, however, differed: they pointed out that the laws of hospitality forbade random slaughter of guests – especially those who'd had too much to drink, and whose words could therefore not be taken seriously – and so Thor had to bite his tongue as Hrungnir left. The two of them, though, agreed that three days later (by which time Hrungnir would presumably have recovered from his hangover) they would meet for a formal duel at a place called Griottunagard.

The morning after, Hrungnir realized that he had been rather foolish. He consulted some of the other giants as to how he might get out of the duel, and they told him it was impossible. However, they did point out that the formalities of the duel meant that not only did Hrungnir have to do battle with Thor, their two squires had to fight each other: surely it would be easy enough to elect a squire who could make mincemeat out of Thor's squire, Thialfi (see below). This struck Hrungnir as a good idea, and so, not wanting to leave too much to doubt in the contest between the squires, he gave orders that a nine-mile-tall clay giant called Mokerkialfi should be constructed to fight against Thialfi. Into this vast edifice the giants placed a mare's

heart – a human heart would not have been sufficient – but they became nervous when they noticed that even this powerful organ was fluttering with worry.

Hrungnir had become less worried. He was vast and had a shield, club, heart and skull made of stone; his squire was even vaster and, it would seem, twice as invulnerable. The duel proved in fact to be a walkover, because Thialfi had little difficulty in slaughtering Mokerkialfi and Thor even less in killing Hrungnir. However, the giant held up his stone club in an attempt to ward off the thrown hammer of Thor; the club shattered into millions of pieces, which can now be found all over the world as fragments of flint. One of these bits of rock flew into Thor's forehead. At the time it caused the god to collapse forward into unconsciousness, but fortunately his descending hand brought down his hammer, Miölnir, on Hrungnir's head, and —— the giant died as a result.

One of the giant's legs fell over Thor. Luckily the god's son Magni strolled up and – although still aged only three – was able to remove the hugely heavy leg. Thor rewarded his son by giving him the steed Gullfaxi.

And that was the end of that adventure – except for the problem of the shard of stone in Thor's forehead. The Aesir tried everything to get it out, and finally thought they would succeed in doing so when they secured the service of a powerful sorceress called Groa. However, for reasons previously described, even this proved of no avail.

Thor had two regular attendants: the boy Thialfi (who became important, as we've seen) and a girl, Roskva. The god gained them in a rather despicable way. He and Loki were wandering the world when the two gods decided that they would like lodging for the night. They took this from a very poor peasant couple, who produced a supper that was in no way big enough to satisfy Thor's huge appetite. The god therefore killed their only two

LEFT *Icelandic bronze statuette, dating from about the year 1000, showing Thor with his hammer.*

goats – although he told the family that, should they leave all the bones untouched and put them back into the empty skins of the animals, things would be all right in the morning. This would have been an honest enough scheme had not Loki encouraged the son of the house, Thialfi, to break one of the bones and lick out its marrow. The next day Thor touched the two heaps of skin and bones with his hammer and suddenly there were two living goats again.

One of them was lame, though, and this made Thor very angry – angry enough to threaten to slaughter the entire family, even though they had given him hospitality for the night. In order to spare all of their lives, the peasant offered Thor Thialfi, the culprit, and his sister Roskva as slaves for eternity. Thor accepted at once.

The gaining of these two slaves occurred during a venture of Thor's to Jotunheim, the land of the giants; the gods had become concerned that the giants were beginning to be too impertinent. Taking the two children with them, Thor and Loki quested on into Jotunheim, their destination a place called Utgard. That night they were cold and lonely, and were only too happy to discover a house where they could sleep; the house was rather strange, but they didn't mind that – all they wanted was somewhere they could sleep. However, sleep was not as easy to come by as they had hoped, because every now and then the ground trembled. Finally the two gods retreated into an annexe of the house, and there at last they were able to sleep in peace.

The reason that the ground had been shaking became obvious to them the following morning when they stumbled, bleary-eyed, out of the strangely shaped house. Nearby a giant was snoring. He almost immediately registered their less than friendly stares and awoke; he reached around him for something that he had lost during the night and soon found it. It was a glove – and also it was the oddly shaped house in which Thor and Loki had spent the night. The annexe which they had finally discovered was the thumb of the glove.

The giant told the two gods that his name was Skrymir; he, too, was on the way to Utgard, and he would gladly show them the way. He offered to share his provisions with them and they readily accepted, because they were running low on supplies. The giant showed what he meant by 'sharing' when he scooped up their pathetically thin bag and simply popped it into

LEFT *Arthur Rackham's conception of Thor, produced as one of his illustrations to Wagner's* Das Rheingold. *Wagner was retelling the older German versions of the Norse myths, and so in the opera the god is named Donner rather than Thor.*

his own. All day long the two gods and the two children suffered the tortures of hunger as they did their best to keep up with Skrymir. Things didn't improve that evening, despite the fact that the giant tossed them his bag of provisions: even the mighty Thor was unable to get the damned thing open.

Brought to a pitch of fury by this and by Skrymir's snoring, Thor came as near to rational argument as he usually did. His first piece of witty repartee was to crash Miölnir down on Skrymir's forehead with a mighty blow; the giant responded by half-waking and enquiring if a forest leaf might have landed on his brow. Thor, ever the diplomat, waited until the giant was fast asleep once more: this time he brought his hammer down viciously on the top of Skrymir's skull. Again the giant half-awoke, this time enquiring if, perhaps, an acorn had dropped down onto his head. Questions like these did not please Thor, and so the god kept himself awake, loathing the incessant snoring, until it was nearly dawn. Then he crept across to where Skrymir was sleeping and buried Miölnir up to the very hilt in the giant's brains. The giant stirred and wondered if perhaps a bird seated in a branch above him had shat on his head.

Grey with lack of sleep, Thor roused his companions; the god was treated to a discourse from Skrymir about how he (the giant) was a veritable midget in comparison with the denizens of Utgard. Thor's temper was as sweet as might be imagined.

Thanks to Skrymir's guidance, the four of them were able to make their way to Utgard, which was where the giant Utgard-Loki lived. Rather to their surprise they found themselves welcomed by him, although he did make tactless remarks about their diminutive stature. They were heralded into a hall where countless giants and giantesses were feasting.

A challenge was soon set up between Loki and Utgard-Loki (who was, incidentally, no relation to the god). Loki avowed that he could eat more

swiftly than anyone or anything in the nine worlds. The giant nodded and chuckled, and gave orders that a great trough of food should be set up the length of one of the huge tables. Loki was commanded to start eating at one end and Utgard-Loki's champion, Logi, at the other. To his astonishment Loki discovered that, when he reached the midpoint, his rival had devoured not only the food, as Loki had done, but the trough as well.

Thor felt that the honour of the Aesir had to be retrieved, and so he proposed a second contest. He told Utgard-Loki that there was no one in all the nine worlds who could swig so much mead as he could, and so he would like to suggest a drinking contest. He would drain whatever vessel the company could put in front of him. The giant immediately called for a horn of mead and, on its arrival,

RIGHT *Swedish silver pendant representing Thor's hammer, found in a Viking grave at Öländ believed to date from the tenth or eleventh century.*

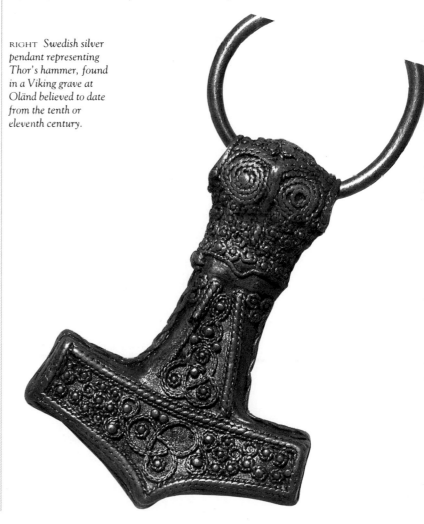

explained that in his hall modest drinkers required three draughts to finish it, reasonable tipplers a couple, and real experts only the one. Thor regarded himself as a real expert and so was surprised to find, having taken a draught so huge that he felt his head would explode, that he had hardly reduced the liquid's level at all. A second attempt made very little more difference. A third, and the horn was still almost full. Thor slumped down in defeat.

Thialfi was then asked to race. His opponent was a boy called Hugi. At his first attempt Thialfi was soundly beaten; in later attempts he found Hugi strolling back to ask if he could offer any help.

RIGHT *Danish silver amulet representing Thor's hammer and dating from perhaps the tenth century.*

Thor offered to show his huge strength, and the giant laughed. He asked the god to try to lift one of the cats of Utgard, which Thor tried with little success. 'All right,' said the giant, 'if that foe proved too much for you, why not have a try against my old nanny, Elli?' Once again Thor proved humiliatingly incapable of putting up even a decent fight. He and Loki – rather surprisingly, in view of the Aesir's disposition to cheat in these affairs – finally admitted that they had been well and truly beaten by the giant's champions. Utgard-Loki smiled and offered them a bed for the night.

The following morning the giant himself escorted the quartet away from his hall. He had to confess, he said, that in many ways he had cheated them. He had taken on the guise of the huge Skrymir and, while pretending to be asleep, had interposed a mountain between Thor's hammer-blows and himself; otherwise he would have been slain – as it was, all the mountains of the worlds showed the scars of the blows. Loki's opponent in the eating competition, Logi, had in fact been fire, than which nothing can eat faster. Thialfi's opponent in the running race, Hugi, was none other than thought – obviously nobody and nothing can hope to race against the speed of thought. The horn out of which Thor had been drinking had been connected with the wide ocean, which, plainly, even this great god could never hope to drain – although he'd managed, creditably, to cause a noticeable drop in the water level. The cat with which Thor had fought had been Jormungand, the World Serpent, which was well known to be unliftable. When Thor had been wrestling old nurse, Elli, he had had little chance because in fact she was old age: no one can hope successfully to resist old age.

Thor would have liked to have exacted vengeance for all these deceptions, and he started to whirl his hammer in preparation. However, Utgard-Loki wisely disappeared, and the thunder-god was never able thereafter to find the giant's hall.

The thunder-god had various other adventures with giants, often involving Loki. The recovery of his hammer from Thrym involved him disguising himself as Freya (*q.v.*). He destroyed Geirrod and his daughters as well as the previously amicable giant Hymir. In fact, it is curious that any of the giant race should show anything other than loathing for this god, so many of them did he slay, yet there are some examples of them being helpful to him – for example, his life would have been forfeited had it not been for the prior assistance of a giantess called Grid.

LEFT *Stone from
Lärbro, Sweden,
currently in the
Museum of National
Antiquities, Stockholm.
In the central panel we
can see Odin's horse
Sleipnir carrying a dead
hero to Valhalla.*

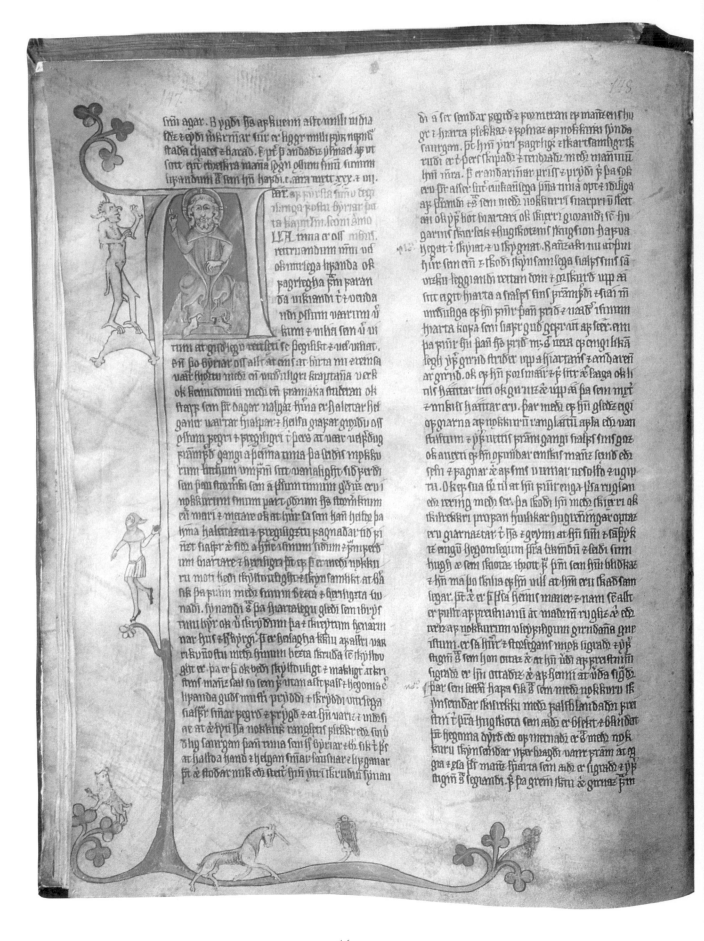

VALI

Vali, the god of eternal light, was conceived with no purpose other than to avenge the death of Balder. A dead prophetess had told Odin that he must mate with the goddess Rind to produce this child, who would grow to adulthood in a single day (quite a number of the lesser deities did this) and then, before he had either washed his face or combed his hair – as the prophetess eloquently put it – slay Hoder; for more details of this prophecy *see* the discussion of Balder earlier in this chapter.

Rind, his mother, is generally taken to have been an earth-goddess. One tale of his conception, possibly tacked on later, portrays her as a mortal – although perhaps, despite her mortal origins, she afterwards became a goddess.

The Rind in this particular tale was the only child of a king called Billing. Her father's country was being threatened by invaders and he was now too old to go to war to repel them, yet she stubbornly refused to take a husband – despite the fact that her beauty had attracted, like iron filings to a magnet, exquisitely handsome suitors from all directions. This was good news for Odin because, in order to avenge the death of Balder, the god had of necessity to sire Vali with Rind. Accordingly, one day Odin, in the guise of a mortal, turned up at Billing's palace offering his services as a military commander. The king, desperate for any help he could get, took him on immediately, and it wasn't very long before the enemies had been repulsed. The triumphant general begged Billing's permission to pay court to his daughter, and there was very little argument. From the father, that is: Rind had other ideas, and sent the grizzled soldier packing.

Odin next appeared as a smith called Rosterus. He could make the most marvellously beautiful brooches and bangles, which delighted all of the court, including Billing and Rind herself. The request for permission to woo being duly granted, the smith tried his luck. The response from Rind was painful to him, to say the least, and he was never seen again at Billing's palace.

The god decided that perhaps middle-aged soldiers and crinkled smiths were not quite what Rind had in mind as a future husband, so next time he turned up as a mighty-thewed warrior – but with the same result. Odin was annoyed at being constantly hit about the head and worse, and so he levelled at her a runestaff, chanting vicious magic spells. Rind collapsed at this onslaught and, by the time she'd revived, the bulky stud had gone. Even after her recovery she was witless. Billing wept for the plight of his daughter, and was much cheered when an old woman arrived at the palace announcing that she alone could bring the lass back to reality. The hag publicly tried a footbath on Rind but without success; there was no other option, she said, but that Rind be put completely under her control. Billing agreed eagerly. Now that this wish had been granted the old woman revealed that in fact she was Odin in disguise. Rind, over whom whom he had been given total mastery, had no choice but to have sex with him – and thereby Vali could be conceived. (The rape theme recurs disturbingly often in the Norse legends.)

An important point about Vali is that he will survive Ragnarok. He is one of the comparatively few gods who will do so.

Valhalla

Valhalla was the hall of Odin to which the warriors slaughtered in battle – the Einheriar – were brought so that they could enjoy a glorious afterlife. The word 'enjoy' is used cautiously, because few of us now would find much pleasure in the daytime activity of the Einheriar. Each morning they had to dress in their armour and then do combat in the plain before Valhalla, perhaps enjoying the lethal blows they dealt to their fellows but, presumably, suffering over and over again the agonies of the lethal blows that had been dealt by others to themselves. Each evening they were brought back to life, free from any of the mutilations they might have suffered, and came back to Valhalla to engage in feats of consuming limitless food and mead. So much did this 'lifestyle' appeal to the Vikings that, apparently, warriors who had failed to be slain during their active years would fall on their own spears in order to qualify for inclusion among the company of the Einheriar.

BELOW *A detail of an eighth-century stela from Lillbjärs, Sweden, showing a valkyrie offering a horn of mead to a slain warrior as he arrives at Valhalla.*

The boiled meat they ate came from a huge boar called Saehrimnir, and the supplies were unending because, even though the boar was slaughtered each day by Valhalla's cook, Andhrimnir, it would be reborn in time to be slaughtered again for their next meal. The mead came from the udder of Odin's goat Heidrun, who supplied more than enough for the Einheriar, who drank it from the skulls of their enemies. Presumably an additional delight of Valhalla was that no one ever suffered a hangover, because the quantities of mead drunk by the dead warriors were colossal. The servants at these gargantuan feasts were the Valkyries, sumptuous young women whose favours were, one gathers, readily available to the bold – although at the same time they remained everlastingly virginal.

BELOW *Nineteenth-century book illustration by Gaston Bussière showing a highly romanticised image of a valkyrie. In the original legends the valkyries might be beautiful and free* with their favours once dead warriors had reached Valhalla, but on the battlefield they were regarded as possessed of the utmost sadistic bloodthirstiness.*

RIGHT *A romanticised vision from a nineteenth-century book of the valkyries carrying off slain heroes to Valhalla. The lowermost hero appears to have attracted the attention of a nubile valkyrie through having incurred a fatal hangover.*

RIGHT *Figures in silver from Swedish Viking graves. The one on the right, dating from an eleventh-century grave, shows a stereotyped valkyrie holding up a drinking horn. The one on the left, dating from the previous century, shows a horseman — presumably the warrior himself riding to Valhalla.*

Our modern image of the Valkyries has been coloured by performances of the operas of Richard Wagner: we think of them as objects of ridicule, buxom and garbed in a costume which goes largely unnoticed except for their precarious metal brassières. In fact, according to the Norse, they were far from that. They were beautiful and desirable, yes, and they were also unbelievably sadistic – except to the Einheriar. Assistants to Tyr, the god of war, they rode on their panting steeds – sometimes wolves – across the skies above battlefields, swooping to pluck the dead from the ground and bring them to Valhalla. Sometimes they took monstrous forms and poured rains of blood down over the land or rowed a ship across the skies through a torrent of blood. In one account they are described as seated on a battlefield weaving a tapestry from human intestines, using an arrow for a shuttle and men's heads to weigh down the ends of their gory cords.

Valkyries are connected with several of the heroes, whose wives they became. There is a great deal of evidence that the myth of their existence had some basis in reality (or perhaps the myth gave rise to the reality), and that priestesses did indeed attend Teutonic armies, including the Norse, with the responsibility of, after a battle, selecting those prisoners to be killed and choosing the manner of their death. This latter was generally not pleasant, but could be regarded as an honour conveyed by the victors upon the vanquished. One delightful tribute the Norse made to those who had been bested in battle, but who were regarded as particularly valiant foes, was the Eagle. The prisoner was held face-downwards and split open along the backbone. His ribs were then splayed outwards and his lungs dragged away to form a canopy over them. It was regarded as a particular sign of valour if the victim showed no sign of pain during all this.

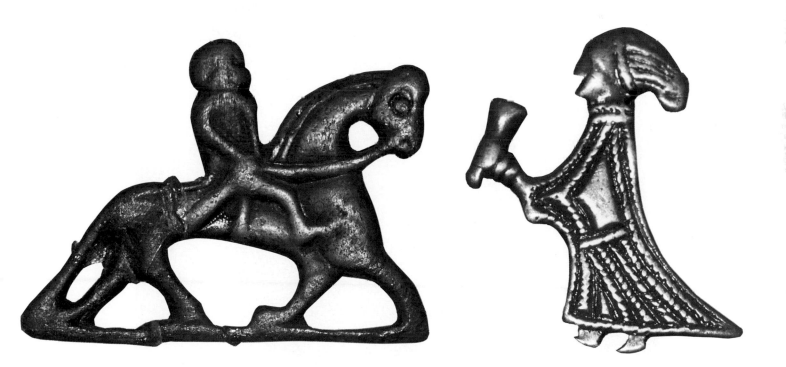

Tales of the
Valkyries

BRUNHILD

The tale of Brunhild is a very muddled one, with several mutually incompatible strands. We shall pick our way through it as best we can.

After the hero Sigurd (q.v.) had stolen Fafnir's gold he rode on until he came to a hall set high on a mountain. Inside it there was a beautiful woman asleep, dressed in full armour. Instinctively knowing what to do in such circumstances, Sigurd took his sword and cut away her armour, at which point she awoke and told him that her name was Brunhild and that she was a Valkyrie.

This is where the tale starts to become confused. According to the Prose Edda, Sigurd then continued on his way as if nothing had happened until he came to the palace of a king called Giuki, one of whose daughters was Gudrun (q.v.). (There is a version that states that Sigurd had agreed to marry Brunhild but that, after he had come to Giuki's court, Queen Grimhild determined that he should marry her daughter and so used magic to erase all memory of his earlier betrothal.) Sigurd married Gudrun and became the blood-brother of two of Giuki's sons, Gunnar and Högni. Sigurd and the two brothers went to ask a king of the Huns called Atli if he would con-sent to the marriage of his sister Brunhild to Gunnar. (You were forewarned that this would be difficult to unravel.) This sister lived in a hall called Hindarfiall which was surrounded by a curtain of flame; it was well known that she would not consider marriage to any man who was not prepared to ride through the flame. Gunnar's horse refused the challenge, but then Sigurd had a ready answer: he would take the shape of Gunnar and, on his own much braver steed called Grani, endure the fire to capture the hand of Brunhild on Gunnar's behalf. This he did with little difficulty. The beautiful maid took one look at him and was much in love. Sigurd, however, being an honourable man, although he slept with Brunhild did not make love with her – a fact which she must have found rather perplexing. In the morning Sigurd gave her as a wedding gift the ring that Loki had taken as part of Andvari's gold: bearing in mind that this ring was accursed, the wedding gift might perhaps have been better chosen. Then Sigurd rode back to join the two brothers and exchanged forms with Gunnar, who thereafter became Brunhild's loving husband.

There was a certain degree of tension between Brunhild and Gudrun, because both of them were essentially in love with the same man. In one instance the two of them were washing their hair in the river and conducting a boasting contest about the prowess

RIGHT *A carving on a cart recovered from a ninth-century ship burial at Vestfold, Norway, shows on the left how Gunnar met his end. He was condemned by Atli to be cast into a pit of snakes. In the pit, his hands being bound, he played on his harp using his toes, and thereby reduced all but one of the serpents to tranquility. This last serpent – Atli's mother in disguise – gave the fatal bite.*

of their respective husbands. Brunhild bragged about Gunnar's bravery in riding through the wall of flame, and Gudrun broke it to her that the man who had performed this feat had in fact been Sigurd.

Brunhild was not at all delighted to hear this news, and decided that Sigurd's deception should be avenged. She tried to persuade the brothers Gunnar and Högni to kill Sigurd, but they refused, delegating the task instead to their brother Guttorm. Guttorm lost his life while killing Sigurd and Sigurd's infant son; as Gudrun expressed her grief Brunhild laughed mockingly. Soon, however, Brunhild changed her mind: she killed herself in order to be placed on Sigurd's funeral pyre.

There are many variant versions of this story. According to some, Brunhild and Sigurd did not behave quite as decorously as described above when Sigurd had come into Hindarfiall, the result being a daughter called Auslag. The child was still very young when her parents died and so was looked after by her grandfather, Giuki. However, a revolution drove him from his kingdom and he was forced to wander the world as a minstrel, bearing a harp in which was hidden his lovely granddaughter. In the end he was murdered by peasants who thought that there was gold in his harp and who were very disappointed to discover the girl-child. Because they thought she was a deaf-mute they reared her as a skivvy, not noticing that she was growing up to be an exceptionally fair young woman. At last a Viking called Ragnar Lodbrog saw her and fell in love. He had to travel away for a year, killing people in order to attain glory, but when he returned he took her as his bride – and so she became the queen of Denmark.

Another possible interpretation of the story is that Brunhild was initially a mortal. Sigurd, on his death, was clearly destined to be taken to Valhalla. Her love for him was so great that she wished to follow him there, becoming a Valkyrie – and the only

55

RIGHT *An
illustration from FL
Spence's* Rhine
Legends *(1915)
showing Odin and
Brunhild.*

way that she could do this was to kill herself and be consumed beside him on his pyre. Yet another version of her story describes her as a king's daughter rudely plucked by Odin from the mortal world to become the leader of all the Valkyries, a position of honour that meant she became, in effect, Odin's own daughter. Obviously there is always the possibility that these legends are confusing two quite different Brunhilds, one a mortal and the other a Valkyrie. The variation of the tale rendered in Wagner's *Ring* cycle is a far later version, bearing little relation to the Norse legends.

GUDRUN

As with Brunhild, the tales of Gudrun are very confused: it is likely that they are confabulations of legends about two quite separate Gudruns, one a mortal and the other a Valkyrie. The exploits of the 'mortal Gudrun' are discussed above: she was the wife of Sigurd and, as such, was probably less poorly treated in the legends than might have been expected of the Norse, who attributed to women a great many powers and guiles, few of which were very flatteringly portrayed. Like Brunhild, Gudrun may have started off as a mortal and then been transformed into a Valkyrie.

The son of Sigmund and Borghild was called Helgi, and he was a very brave warrior. Gudrun, as she swooped over a battlefield where Helgi and Sinfiotli were fighting with the Hundings, was much taken by the young man. She accordingly descended to Earth and threw herself before him, offering her all. Helgi thanked her but, as it were, he had this battle to fight first: they could be betrothed but the consummation would have to wait a while. After the battle there was only one of the Hundings still standing – a youth called Dag, who was given his freedom on the condition that he would not

seek to carry on the vendetta any longer. Dag agreed to this but then betrayed his oath and slew Helgi.

Gudrun's grief was great; not surprisingly, she laid a curse on Dag. She discovered that the dead Helgi, buried in his mound, was calling for her incessantly, and so she went to him. She found that he was still bleeding prodigiously, and he told her that this was because of her continuing grief: every time she shed a tear, he shed a matching drop of blood. From then on she kept back her tears.

The loving couple were soon reunited. Helgi was gathered to Valhalla and Gudrun joined him there. He became a leader of the armies of the dead warriors, the Einheriar; she, in order to help him, returned to her role as a Valkyrie so that she could bring as many slain warriors as possible to swell the ranks of his armies.

The rest of the tale of the 'mortal Gudrun' is less edifying. While Brunhild had so graphically displayed her love for Sigurd by immolating herself upon his pyre, Gudrun was not prepared to do likewise, so she and her daughter Swanhild fled to the court of a king called Elf. His queen was Thora, and

RIGHT *Arthur
Rackham's typically
romantic image of
Brunhild. Warlike the
valkyries might be, but
there is little to make us
believe that the Vikings
saw them as beautiful,
clean-limbed maidens
like this, rather, they
were hideous creatures,
akin to vampires or the
Irish tripartite death-
goddess The Morrigan,
when they visited
earthly battlefields to
carry off the souls of the
dead.*

FAR RIGHT *Detail of a cross slab found at Michael, Isle of Man, Britain, dating from the late tenth or early eleventh century; the slab is called 'Joalf's Slab'. The Viking depicted is bearing a spear and a round shield.*

RIGHT, *A detail from a stone-carved cross, from Middleton, North Yorkshire, Britain, dating from about the tenth century, showing a Norse warrior laid out for burial. The cross was, of course, a Christian artefact, the burial a pagan one. This mixture of paganism with Christianity became increasingly a characteristic of the late Viking period, until eventually the new religion took over almost completely.*

soon Gudrun and Thora were close friends. However, this situation didn't last too long, because Atli, king of the Huns, was demanding to be avenged upon Gunnar; the latter, now king, was eager to avoid war and so he told Atli that he could marry his sister Gudrun. The marriage was eventually performed, much to Gudrun's disgust: she loathed Atli. In due course she murdered the sons he had sired upon her and served bits of them up to him in a banquet: their skulls were used for goblets, their blood was mixed into the wine, and the meat was their roasted hearts. Then Gudrun revealed the truth to Atli before setting fire to his palace and dying with him and his cronies in the flames.

Swanhild, Gudrun's daughter, met an equally unsavoury end. A king called Ermenrich wanted her as a wife and sent his son Randwer to fetch her. When they reached Ermenrich's palace, however, a lying and treacherous servant called Sibich claimed that, during the journey, Randwer had seduced Swanhild. At Ermenrich's order Randwer was hanged and Swanhild sentenced to be trampled to death by wild horses. Early attempts to carry out this execution failed because of Swanhild's exquisite beauty: the horses simply refused to harm her. In the end she was covered with a blanket to shield her beauty from the horses, and so she lost her life.

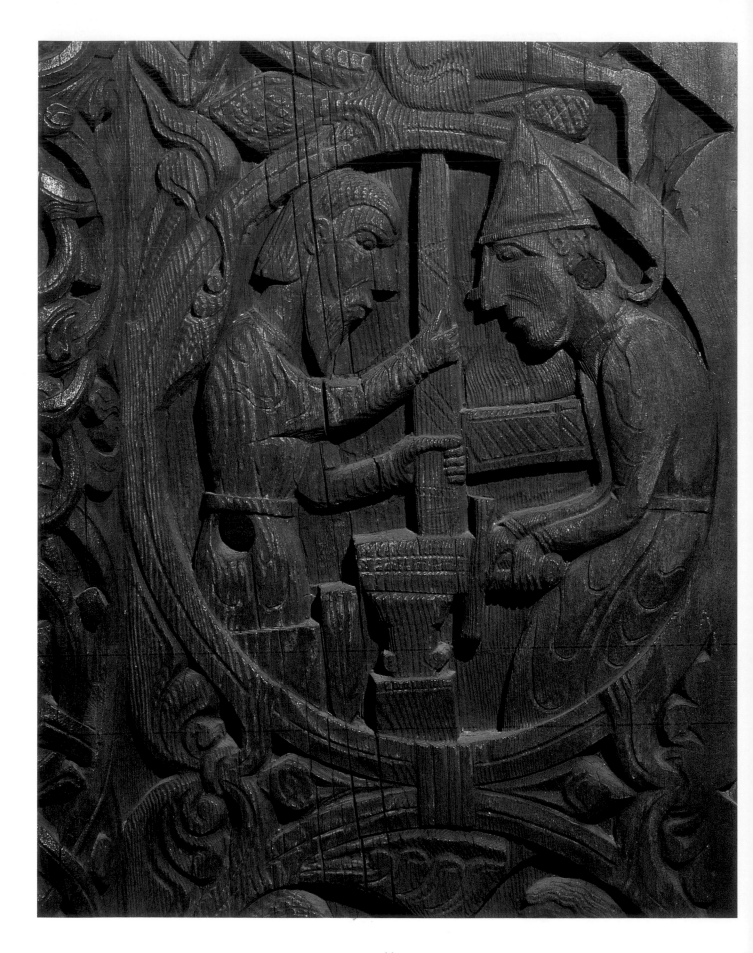

Tales of Heroes

LEFT *Detail from a twelfth- or thirteenth-century wooden portal at Hylestad Church, Norway, showing the dwarf Regin reforging the sword Sigurd had been given by his father.*

FRITHIOF

Frithiof was the son of Thorsten (q.v.) and Ingeborg. Early in his life he was given out to a man called Hilding for fostering (this was a not uncommon practice among the Vikings). Hilding later became the foster-father of a girl who was also called Ingeborg; she was the daughter of Thorsten's great friend King Belé. The two children grew up together and, predictably, fell in love with each other; but Hilding forbade them to marry, pointing out that Ingeborg was a princess while Frithiof was merely the son of a hero. Frithiof took this as well as might be expected – in other words, not very.

Belé's heirs were his sons Halfdan and Helgé, neither of whom were particularly popular; Frithiof, on the other hand, was very popular indeed – even with Belé himself. After Halfdan and Helgé had taken over the throne from their father, Frithiof decided to retire from public life, although he pined for Ingeborg.

One Spring, however, Halfdan and Helgé came to visit him and they brought with them their sister. Ingeborg and Frithiof were instantly, once again, madly and passionately in love. After the royal party had left, Frithiof decided to pluck up his courage and follow them in order to beg the two kings, his former playmates, to let him marry their sister. When he came to them, sitting on their father's barrow, Helgé told him that he was not good enough for Ingeborg, being only a peasant's son; he could, however, if he wanted, become one of Helgé's bondsmen. Aroused to a level beyond mere tetchiness, Frithiof drew his sword and sliced Helgé's shield in two. Then he went home, much disgruntled.

Ingeborg was beautiful, and the news of this spread widely, so that princely suitors sent messengers from many lands. One of these was a king called Sigurd Ring, a widower of great age. Ingeborg having, of course, no voice in any of these discussions, Helgé asked various seers and seeresses whether or not there was any chance that the marriage would be successful; Halfdan, more relevantly, wondered if the old man, Sigurd Ring, would be able to – um – give Ingeborg the full joys of marriage. The limp joke came to the ears of Sigurd Ring, who became enraged and announced publicly that he planned to wage war on Halfdan and Helgé. The response of the two kings was less than heroic: they instantly sent Hilding to ask Frithiof to command their armies in an endeavour to repel the threat. Frithiof's reply was that he had been so offended by their earlier remarks that he had little interest in sorting things out for them. Halfdan and Helgé decided that their best course of action was to give in to Sigurd Ring and to give him the hand of their sister, Ingeborg.

Frithiof was not quite so sure that that was the end of the story. He discovered that Ingeborg was pining in a religious house devoted to Balder, and so he went there. It was taboo to speak in this place, but they spoke anyway, and over many days, knowing that Ingeborg's brothers were away. The brothers returned, though; to Frithiof's request that they might think about his offer to lead their armies against Sigurd Ring the two of them – notably Helgé – remarked that they were much more interested in whether or not Frithiof and Ingeborg had been talking with each other in the grove (or monastery) devoted to Balder. Helgé pressed the question: had Frithiof and Ingeborg spoken with each other? There was a long silence before Frithiof replied that, yes, he had.

His sentence was banishment. Ingeborg declined to follow him to the sunny lands he knew lay to the south; she reckoned that now her father was dead she ought to do what her brothers told her.

Helgé was not content with Frithiof's sentence of banishment: he wanted the man dead. The king there-

RIGHT *Sigmund and Signy – a nineteenth-century book illustration.*

fore summoned up a couple of witches and asked them to send a storm out to sea so that Frithiof's ship, and all on board her, should be sunk. The witches did their best, but Frithiof, chanting a merry lay, dissuaded the elements from killing him and his crew. In this way they all came to the Orkney Islands. The natives were not much pleased by this, obviously, but Frithiof defeated the berserker, Atlé, whom they sent to challenge him. Frithiof also made friends, in due course, with the king of the Orkneys, Angantyr.

After many months Frithiof came home, only to discover that his hall had been burnt to the ground on the orders of Helgé. Also, he was given the news by Hilding that Ingeborg had been married to Sigurd Ring. He carried out various acts of slaughter and then set sail for Greece, where he lived for some years. He finally returned to the court of Sigurd Ring in the guise of a beggar, a role that he maintained only as long as it took for him to kill one of the courtiers. Sigurd Ring, very decently, did not have him executed

for this crime but instead asked him to doff his disguise; this Frithiof did, thereby meeting the appealing eye of Ingeborg. The hero then had too much to drink, watched with approval by Sigurd Ring. The two men became great friends, and that was the end, for a while, of Frithiof's lust for Ingeborg.

Sigurd Ring died, and at last Frithiof and Ingeborg were free to marry. Helgé accidentally killed himself. Halfdan, on the other hand, swore an oath of friendship with Frithiof, and the two men remained friends until the end of their lives.

SIGMUND

S igmund was the twin brother of the beautiful woman Signy; they were the last two children of Volsung. Sigmund was the only one of all the brothers to realize that Signy didn't want to marry Siggeir, the king of the Goths; however, Odin had a similar idea and turned up for the wedding feast, throwing a sword into the heart of the Branstock, a great oak that grew up through Volsung's hall; according to Odin, whoever was able to remove the sword would become a great hero.

Siggeir, the recent groom, tried to pull the sword from the tree but without success; Volsung was no luckier. Then Sigmund's nine elder brothers had a try, all of them unsuccessfully. Finally Sigmund himself had a go, and the sword immediately slid out of its wooden scabbard; the comparison with King Arthur is very obvious.

King Siggeir offered to buy the weapon but Sigmund refused; it was at this point that the king determined to exterminate Sigmund and all of his kin, including Signy. As Siggeir slept, Signy told Volsung that her new husband was up to no good, but Volsung wouldn't believe her. A while later Volsung sent a fleet of vessels to Siggeir's kingdom; he and all of his war-

LEFT *Reconstruction of a Viking helmet found at Middleton Cross, Yorkshire, Britain.*

riors were murdered. Sigmund himself was lucky enough to escape, although he had to give up his magical sword; he and his brothers were then sentenced to death. Signy was distraught at this, and asked that the death penalty be rescinded; the result was that their sentence was commuted to being tied up to trees in the forest, there to be eaten by wild animals, while Signy was locked up in Siggeir's palace. All of the brothers died except Sigmund; this was because Signy had the idea of smearing honey on his face, so that the wild creatures of the forest licked this away rather than eating him. The beast that attacked him that night attempted a french kiss, thrusting its tongue into Sigmund's mouth; he bit back forcefully, killing it.

Signy arrived to rejoice about her brother's survival; he, for his part, went off to become a smith, operating out of a remote part of the forest.

That wasn't the end of the story, though. Signy concluded that the sons she bore by Siggeir were wimps and decided to send them to Sigmund for a bit of bracing. The test to which he put them was to knead some bread and not notice that, within the dough, there was a viper. The first son of Signy either noticed it and fled or was killed by Sigmund; the second got the same treatment. Signy despaired of the third son she might have by Siggeir, and so she decided to have one by Sigmund instead; she called on a beautiful witch, adopted her form, and slept with her brother. The resulting son was Sinfiotli. He showed himself to be better than his stepbrothers because, when baking bread, he simply baked the viper along with all the rest.

Sigmund and Sinfiotli became boon companions and soon began to rush around Scandinavia killing people, in the typical manner of heroes. In one of their adventures they became werewolves. They discovered two men sleeping and, on the wall, a pair of wolfskins. Father and son immediately donned these, wondering what it would feel like. Moments later they were werewolves that ran through the forest and ate anyone who came in their way. The two got so excited that they started to fight each other; Sigmund killed Sinfiotli. The father then watched as two weasels fought with each other; one killed the other but then restored it to life by laying on its breast a particular leaf; Sigmund followed suit and brought his son Sinfiotli back to life. The two of them realized that they'd been a bit stupid risking their lives as werewolves, and so as soon as possible they shed their skins and reverted to human form.

Sigmund and Sinfiotli now decided that they would exact their revenge on Siggeir. They went to Siggeir's hall, where they were soon discovered by two of Signy's youngest children; their mother told Sigmund to cut off the children's heads but he refused, so she did it herself.

Sigmund and Sinfiotli were captured and sentenced to death by Siggeir; their punishment was that they should be buried alive in a mound, separated by a wall. The mound was almost complete when Signy came along and threw at Sinfiotli's feet a bale of hay. He assumed that it might contain a loaf of bread, but actually it contained Sigmund's magical sword; as quick as thought Sinfiotli hacked an exit from the burial tomb.

The two heroes immediately rushed back to Volsung's hall and built up a great pile of straw all around it. They set fire to this and then stood at the gate refusing to let anyone escape but the women. An exception was Signy, whom they would have allowed out; she apparently preferred to burn alive as a penance for her infanticide and incestuous adultery.

Sigmund went on to marry the fair princess Borghild and then the equally fair princess Hiordis. Unfortunately a certain King Lygni likewise wanted to marry Hiordis; when Sigmund became the successful suitor Lygni raised an army. In the ensuing war Sigmund slew hundreds but was eventually killed himself.

Sigmund's son was the hero Sigurd (*q.v.*).

SIGURD

Hiordis was pregnant when her husband Sigmund (*q.v.*) was slain. She was lucky enough, however, to meet up with a benevolent Viking called Elf, who asked her to marry him and promised to look after her forthcoming child as if he were its real father. The child arrived and Elf gave him the name Sigurd. In the Germanic version of the legends Sigurd was called Siegfried.

Sigurd's education was entrusted to an infinitely wise man called Regin, and so the boy learned considerable wisdom – music, diplomacy, the carving of runes, smithery, warfare, etc. On attaining adulthood Sigurd was given permission to choose from his stepfather's stable any warhorse he would like. On his way to make the selection Sigurd was met by Odin, who told him that the best means of choice was to drive all of Elf's horses into a nearby river and then pick the one that retained its feet the best in the current. This Sigurd did, and as a result he gained the horse Greyfell, a descendant of Odin's horse Sleipnir.

One day Regin told him of the cursed treasure of Andvari, now guarded by the dragon Fafnir, and asked him if he would be willing to do battle with Fafnir in order to recover the gold and avenge the crime. Sigurd agreed, and so Regin set out to forge for him an invincible sword. His first two attempts were unsuccessful, Sigurd being able to shatter the swords by crashing them down on an anvil. Then Sigurd remembered the sword of his father, Sigmund, the fragments of which were still kept by Hiordis. From those fragments was forged a mighty blade that, when crashed down on the anvil, made great gouges in it. Regin and Sigurd then set sail for the land of the Volsungs. On the way they picked up Odin, although they didn't realize who this stranger was.

RIGHT *As Regin sleeps, Sigurd roasts the heart of the dwarfish smith's brother, who became the dragon Fafnir. This is a detail from a twelfth- or thirteenth-century carved wooden portal at Hylestad Church in Norway.*

LEFT *Details from a twelfth- or thirteenth-century wooden portal at Hylestad Church, Norway, showing the dwarf Regin reforging the sword Sigurd had been given by his father.*

RIGHT *Part of a Viking
cross found at Andreas,
Isle of Man, Britain. At
top left we can see
Sigurd roasting Fafnir's
heart.*

BELOW RIGHT *The
'Waterfall of the Gods'
in Iceland. According to
legend, Thorsten, on
being converted to
Christianity about
AD 1000, threw his
pagon idols over these
falls.*

Sigurd killed Lygni, the killer of his father, and then moved on, with Regin, to kill Fafnir. Again Odin helped him, this time pointing out that the dragon daily used the same path in order to quench his thirst at a nearby river: all that Sigurd had to do was to lie in wait. The operation was a complete success. Regin asked Sigurd to cut out the dragon's heart, barbecue it and serve it up as a meal, and Sigurd immediately agreed to the request. During the roasting Sigurd at one stage touched the heart with his fingers to see if it were ready yet; the hot meat stung his fingers, and he put them to his lips, immediately finding that he could understand the talk of the birds. They were saying to each other that Regin planned to kill him, and that he would be best advised to kill the sage at once and himself devour the dragon's heart and blood, then to claim the treasure. This Sigurd did. He then awoke Brunhild (*q.v.*) from her timeless sleep and became her betrothed. Unfortunately, he then became enamoured of Gudrun (*q.v.*), a daughter of the king of the Nibelungs, and forgot all about Brunhild. Sigurd had kept some of Fafnir's heart, and at his wedding to Gudrun he gave her a little to eat; he also became a blood-brother of her brothers Gunnar and Högni. Gunnar determined to marry Brunhild, with the results seen. Guttorm, the third son of the king of the Nibelungs, was deputed to slay Sigurd, and succeeded, although he lost his own life in doing so. Brunhild shared her one-time lover's funeral pyre.

THORSTEN

Thorsten was one of the nine sons of the hero Viking (*q.v.*) by his second marriage and a survivor of the war with the sons of Viking's great friend Njorfe. The war started when one of Njorfe's sons, during a game of ball, treacherously hit out at one of Viking's sons, who later killed him.

Thorsten became a pirate. He encountered one of the two surviving sons of Njorfe, Jokul, who seems to have been a rather unpleasant piece of work: he had killed the king of Sogn, banished the kingdom's prince, Belé, and turned the princess Ingeborg into an old hag. Jokul used evil magic in attempts to kill Thorsten, but was unsuccessful – in large part thanks to the help of the seeming hag, whom Thorsten agreed to marry in thanks for her assistance. The hero restored Belé to his rightful throne and was delighted to discover that Ingeborg was in fact a beautiful young maiden.

Thorsten, Belé and another hero called Angantyr had many adventures together. They recovered a ship called Ellida that had once been given to Viking by the god Aegir (*q.v.*). They conquered the Orkney Isles, of which Angantyr became the king, although he pledged himself to pay an annual tribute to Belé. Then Thorsten and Belé regained from a pirate called Soté a magic arm-ring that had been forged by Völund (*q.v.*).

Thorsten and Ingeborg had a son called Frithiof (*q.v.*), who himself became a hero.

VIKING

Viking was a grandson of a Norwegian king called Haloge; according to some versions of the mythology Haloge was in fact the god Loki. Whatever the truth of this, Viking was born on an island called Bornholm, in the Baltic Sea. By the time he had reached the age of 15 he was so strong and huge that rumours of him reached Sweden and in particular a princess called Hunvor. At the time Hunvor was being pestered by the attentions of a giant. Pausing only to collect from his father a magic sword called Angurvadel, Viking sailed to Sweden and did battle with the giant. He would have married Hunvor there and then but it was considered that he was too young. He therefore sailed around the North Sea for some years, being tormented by the relatives of the dead

In the whalebone carvings on the early-eighth-century Franks Casket, now in the British Museum, we find a delicious mix of Norse and Christian mythologies. RIGHT *In this section we see, on the left, Völund's smithy and, on the right, the Adoration of the Magi.*

giant and befriended by a man called Halfdan; in due course Viking married Hunvor and Halfdan married a servant of hers called Ingeborg.

Over the next few years Viking and Halfdan led raids to other countries during which they took great pleasure in slaughtering, preferably females whom they first raped. Nevertheless, they were faithful to their wives; such is the way of Norse mythology. They also made friends, after a long war, with a king called Njorfe.

Hunvor died; Viking put out their son Ring to a foster-father and then remarried. He and his new wife had nine sons; Njorfe and *his* wife had the same number. Despite the fact that their fathers had sworn all the oaths of friendship, the sons sustained a long-term antagonism between the two families. Much of the time this took an innocent enough form: as far as one can work out from the legends, the two sets of lads merely met each other on the Norse equivalent of a

football pitch. However, one of Njorfe's sons committed an overly 'cynical' foul on one of Viking's sons, so the latter killed him. This murder infuriated Viking, and thus he banished the boy; the other brothers told their father that they would follow him into exile. The eldest of these sons was Thorsten; to him Viking gave the sword Angurvadel.

Njorfe's sons were not satisfied by this, and followed Viking's sons into the faraway land where they hid. There was a great battle, with the result that only two of Viking's sons – Thorsten and Thorer – and two of Njorfe's sons – Jokul and another – survived. These two pairs swore undying hatred for each other, so Viking sent his own two sons to the court of Halfdan. Thorsten had adventures of his own, during one of which he killed Jokul.

VÖLUND

Völund is well known as Wayland or Weland the Smith; under the former name he turns up, for example, as a character in Walter Scott's novel *Kenilworth* (1821). His brothers were called Egil and Slagfinn.

One day the three brothers came across three Valkyries – Alvit, Olrun and Svanhvit – swimming in a river, and immediately raped them, having stolen the Valkyries' swan plumage so that they were no longer able to leave the Earth. For nine years the three maidens remained with their captors, but then they were able to recover their plumage and return to Valhalla. This was much mourned by the three brothers, and Egil and Slagfinn set off on a quest to see if they could rediscover their brides. Völund, however, reckoned that their search was futile, and so stayed at home.

Alvit had given him a ring, and he looked on this lovingly. A practised smith, he made 700 other rings exactly like it and tied all 701 of them up in a bundle. One day he discovered that one of the rings had been stolen and he was much cheered, believing that this meant that Alvit had returned to Earth to reclaim it and would soon come back to be his wife again.

That night, however, he was attacked and taken prisoner by the king of Sweden, Nidud, who had confiscated Alvit's ring (giving it to his daughter Bodvild) as well as Völund's magic sword. The hapless smith was incarcerated on an island, his hamstrings being cut so that he could have no hope of escape. There he was forced to labour each and every day at his forge to manufacture weapons and ornaments for the brutal king. Völund's opinion of Nidud was by this time not of the highest, and all the time he plotted escape and revenge. He made himself a pair of wings just like those Alvit had used, so that he could fly to join her in Valhalla.

Nidud brought to Völund one day the smith's magic sword, asking for it to be repaired. Völund pretended to comply, but in fact hid it and returned to Nidud an exact replica. A little afterwards he lured Nidud's sons into his smithy, slaughtered them, used their skulls to make goblets and their teeth and eyes as adornments; these he gave to the royal couple, who received them as precious gifts, little realizing their origins. Having exacted his next revenge by raping Bodvild and repossessing from her his magic ring, he donned the wings he had crafted and flew to Nidud's palace, where he enumerated loudly and at length the king's failings and sins. Nidud called for Völund's brother Egil, who was now his slave, and instructed him to shoot Völund down out of the sky; however, Völund signalled to his brother to aim his arrow at a bladder he clutched that was full of the blood of Nidud's sons. This Egil did, and Nidud assumed that his royal archer had slain the enemy, little realizing that Völund had flown.

Völund then rejoined Alvit and is still living with her and practising his craft: he will continue to do so until Ragnarok.

RIGHT *Made from walrus ivory around 1135–1150 and found on the Isle of Lewis, Scotland, this rook (castle) comes from a Viking chess set. When we think of the Vikings we envisage only mindless slaughter, but in fact they regarded chess as such a fine sport that it could have been their equivalent of football.*

73

GREEK
MYTHOLOGY

Tales of Greek Heroes

Apart from the legendary warriors of Homer's epic poems who fought at Troy, several heroes existed who were the central subjects of lengthy sagas. All exhibited super-human strengths, clearing the world of its troublesome monsters, and generally experienced a number of love affairs.

Heracles and Theseus were contrasted in both art and literature. As a boy, Heracles rejected his education and relied on sheer brute strength in his later encounters with men and monsters. He was deified at death and was later worshipped as a god by military men. Theseus was seen as an educated and civilized version of Heracles and became the hero of Athenian democracy in the 5th century BC. He performed similar super-human tasks as Heracles, but introduced more 'gentlemanly' fighting skills. In art Theseus appears short-haired and clean-shaven, while Heracles, easily recognized by his lion skin and club, sports long, shaggy hair and a beard. Perseus (meaning 'slayer-destroyer'), like Heracles, appears to have represented the earlier, more violent stage of Greek mythology. In art Perseus is usually depicted in the winged sandals and magic hat used on his quest for the head of Medusa.

HERACLES

As King and Queen of Tiryns and Mycenae Perseus and Andromeda had many children, but this tale concerns just two of their sons, Alcaeus and Electryon. Alcaeus had a son named Amphitryon, who married his cousin Alcmene, the daughter of Electryon. Amphitryon wanted to become king, but his uncle Electryon stood in his path so he murdered him; the attempted coup failed and Amphitryon and Alcmene were exiled. They travelled to Thebes where King Creon welcomed them. Alcmene would not sleep with Amphitryon until he had avenged her brothers who had been killed by pirates. He returned in triumph one night and they made love whilst he told her of his adventures. Imagine her surprise when the next day he walked in and told her the same stories all over again, as if for the first time. They called in Teiresias the prophet who told them that Zeus had visited Alcmene in the guise of her husband. Amphitryon was willing to forgive Alcmene, but problems arose when Alcmene became pregnant; the whole Theban court waited to see whether the child would be Amphitryon's or Zeus'.

Meanwhile on Olympus, Zeus boasted that a son of his was about to be born on earth who would be a great ruler. Hera, understandably angry and jealous, sent Eileithyia, goddess of childbirth, to delay Alcmene's labour and speed up the birth of Eurystheus, grandson of Perseus, and great-grandson of Zeus, to ensure his inheritance of the throne of Tiryns in place of Alcmene's child. The next day Alcmene gave birth to twin sons, named Iphicles and Heracles, but no one was able to say whether either was the god's progeny. The problem was solved when Hera sent two snakes into the babies' cots as they slept. Iphicles screamed but, to the surprise of Amphitryon and Alcmene, little

LEFT Heracles in the garden of the Hesperides; *Roman wall-painting from the villa at Oplontis, 1st century* AD. *A sun-tanned Heracles carries his club and looks up at the golden apples; the special tree is marked with a ribbon.*

Heracles took the snakes by the necks and strangled them; there was no doubt that this was a son of Zeus.

Heracles received the normal royal education: his step-father taught him to drive the chariot, and various experts were called in to teach him to fence, wrestle and use the bow and arrow; but Heracles showed little interest in these gentlemanly skills, finding that it was quicker and easier to dispatch his opponent with one blow of the fist or a swing of his club. This rather worried his mortal parents, and they thought that some training in the arts would make him behave a little more gracefully. Orpheus's brother Linus, himself a wonderful musician and teacher, was called in to give Heracles music lessons. Heracles proved to be a slow learner and one day Linus lost his temper and struck him; Heracles angrily brought his lyre down on Linus's head killing him instantly; the boy did not know his own strength, nor where it came from.

Amphitryon thought it would be sensible to send him away from the city for a while and Heracles spent many happy summers on the royal cattle farm. In his spare time he would practise with his bow and arrow on the slopes of Mount Cithaeron; he never missed, but found that there were certain creatures whose skins could not be pierced with arrows, so Heracles would wrestle with them. However, there was one that eluded him, a lion that had been eating the flocks of Thespius, their royal neighbour. To get him in a good mood and to see how strong this young man really was before asking him to kill the lion, Thespius invited Heracles to supper and plied him with gallons of wine. That night Thespius sent all fifty of his daughters to his guest's room; the next morning each swore that Heracles had made love to them, but Heracles could not remember anything. On his way back to Thebes he killed the lion with his own bare hands. Nearing Thebes, he encountered some ambassadors on their way from Orchomenus in Minya to collect their annual tribute from Thebes; Heracles in his anger, cut off their noses and ears, and hanging them round their necks, sent them back home with what he called their tribute.

War followed and Heracles led the Thebans to victory. Creon rewarded him with his daughter Megara.

Heracles had been away on business and several years later on his return to Thebes found that Creon had been murdered by a Euboean called Lycus, who was about to execute Heracles' wife and their children. Heracles killed Lycus, but as he was embracing Megara, Hera never forgetting her grudge, brought a fit of madness upon him, and he killed both his wife and his children. Coming to his senses he saw with horror what he had done and took his impure body away from Thebes and walked to Delphi to seek advice from the Pythian Oracle. She pronounced that to atone for his crime, he must travel to Tiryns and ask King Eurystheus to set him ten trials of his strength and courage. Heracles turned to go with face downcast; humiliated that this weakling of a king, Eurystheus, who sat on the throne which he himself would have held if Hera had not tricked his father Zeus, was to have such power over his fate; but the Pythia called after him that if he suc-ceeded in the ten labours he would achieve immortality. Heracles rose to the challenge and was impatient to begin the first of his labours.

1 The Nemean Lion

Heracles' euphoria faded, however, when he stood in Tiryns before the throne of his rival Eurystheus who smirked and demanded the pelt of the Nemean Lion, one of the monstrous sons of Orthus and Echidna, which had been ravaging the surrounding countryside. On his way to Nemea, Heracles stayed for the night in the hut of a peasant named Molorchus, who, when he heard what Heracles was attempting, offered a sacrifice to him. Heracles told his to delay the sacrifice for a month, after which if he had not returned, the sacrifice should be made to Heracles the Hero; but if he returned in triumph, the sacrifice must be made to Zeus the Saviour.

Molorchus pointed out the long path to the lion's cave and wished him luck. Fifteen days later Heracles could hear its distant roaring for several

RIGHT Heracles and the Nemean Lion; *black-figure* oinochoe *(wine-jug), late 6th century* BC. *Heracles has hung up his quiver and bow on a tree and wrestles with the lion.*

79

hours before he eventually found himself peering through the bushes at a cave with two entrances. Heracles strung his bow and, without making a sound, fitted an arrow; he then flung a rock against the nearest mouth of the cave. Immediately a lion, twice the size of the one he had strangled on mount Cithaeron, leapt out of the cave, roaring and spitting with rage at being disturbed. Heracles let his arrow fly and, true as ever, it found its mark between the eyes of the magnificent beast, but Heracles' heart sank as it bounced straight off again. 'What a wonderful warm and light coat of armour that pelt would make, if Zeus would help me to kill the lion!', thought Heracles. Zeus heard him from Olympus – they were all up there watching – and sent his warlike daughter, Athene of the flashing eyes, down to help. Unknown to Heracles, she gave him new courage and he stepped out into the open, rolling a stone in front of one of the entrances; he entered the other one and slew the lion, strangling it as easily as he had the snakes when he was a baby.

Meanwhile Molorchus was preparing to sacrifice to Heracles the dead hero, it being a month since Heracles had left him. Upon seeing the hero returning with the dead Nemean lion over his shoulder, Molorchus praised Zeus and burnt the sacrifice to the Gatherer of Clouds, reserving the meat for a night of feasting and drinking in celebration of Heracles' victory. The local peasants joined them in dancing well into the night; at last they could work in the fields without fear of the monster.

Eurystheus was annoyed when Heracles entered Tiryns in triumph; he was expecting never to see him again and what is more was terrified when he saw the lion which looked as if it might spring to life at any moment. Eurystheus jumped into a storage jar to hide; Heracles could not conceal his amusement and Eurystheus angrily vowed that Heracles would not be laughing when he heard what his next labour was to be. Hera rewarded the

lion's vain attempts to defy Heracles by setting it as the stars in the heavens known as the constellation Leo.

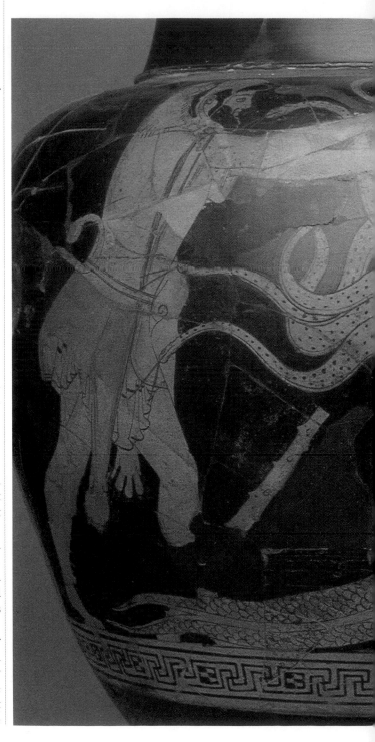

II *The Hydra*

The Hydra was the half-sister of the Nemean Lion, spitefully chosen by Eurystheus as the object of Heracles' second labour as he knew that the Hydra would be yearning to avenge her relative's death. The Hydra had the venomous nature of her father Typhon, who lay crushed by Zeus under Mount Etna, breathing his fires. Heracles left Tiryns, wearing the magnificent pelt of the Nemean lion, its scalp protecting his head like a hood, and as soon as he was clear of the gates, Eurystheus had them bolted and shouted after him from the ramparts that he was to leave any further trophies outside the city walls. Heracles laughed and went on his way in high spirits, accompanied by his nephew Iolaus, who had volunteered to be his charioteer.

The Hydra lived in a pool formed by the freshwater spring Amymone at Lerna. The spring had once been crystal clear and a source of drinking water for the people of Lerna. Now it was polluted and they had to draw their water from a well some distance away, and this meant passing by the Hydra's lair; many of them never returned, finding themselves in one of the jaws of the monster, who would lie in wait for them with its accomplice, Cancer the crab, who would run out and grab the feet of unsuspecting travellers. Heracles approached the pool without fear and fired burning arrows into the cave behind the pool where the Hydra was supposed to live. Out she came, and Heracles was surprised at seeing so many heads, for no one had seen the monster and lived to tell the tale. He did not have time to reflect and found himself hacking away at its heads with his sword; but for every head lost, it immediately grew two more, and he found himself cornered when the giant crab sallied out to bite his ankles. He called to his charioteer Iolaus for help, and the clever youth brought burning torches with which he cauterized the wounded necks as Heracles removed the heads. At last only its huge central head was left; Heracles cut it off with a final blow and buried it beneath a large stone which still lies beside the road outside Lerna. He dipped his arrows into the dead Hydra's poisonous blood and returned to Tiryns in triumph, but Eurystheus refused to acknowledge the labour as one of the ten as Iolaus had helped the hero.

LEFT Heracles and the Hydra; *Athenian red-figure* stamnos *(wine-jar) by the Syleus Painter, early 5th century* BC. *Heracles (left) has laid aside his club to sever the snake-heads while his companion Iolaus cauterizes the open wounds with torches.*

III *The Cerynitian Hind*

For his third labour, Heracles was ordered to capture the golden-horned deer known as the fabulous Cerynitian Hind. The problem for Heracles was that he was to bring it back alive; moreover, the hind was sacred to the goddess Artemis. It had last been seen in the woods around Oenoe in Argolis, a short journey for Heracles. He tracked it down after a year and had little trouble dragging it away with nets. But on the way to Tiryns he encountered Artemis and Apollo who demanded that he return the deer. Heracles blamed Eurystheus, and they let him pass, so long as he did not harm the creature.

IV *The Erymanthian Boar*

Eurystheus now tried to exhaust Heracles, immediately sending him back down to Arcadia to capture alive a huge boar which was terrorizing the shepherds on Mount Erymanthus. On his way Heracles stayed for the night with Centaurs on Mount Pholoe; in the evening they held a banquet, and Pholus, the host, brought out wine for his guest, a drink never before tasted by the Centaurs; the moment they smelt it they became intoxicated and began to cause an uproar. Heracles fought with them and they fled to their mountain homes. The banquet was resumed with soft drinks and Heracles sang of his labours; when he reached the story of the Hydra, Pholus asked to see the poisonous arrows, but still a little drunk, he dropped one on his foot and was dead in an instant. Heracles would one day encounter the Centaurs again.

Heracles had no difficulties in trapping the boar, using the same nets with which the Cerynitian Hind had been ensnared. He was beginning to tire of the labours and when he reached Tiryns, entered the city against the orders of Eurystheus, and threatened to throw the monster into the storage jar in which Eurystheus had fled for refuge.

RIGHT Heracles hurls the Erymanthian Boar at Eurystheus; *Athenian black-figure amphora, mid 6th century BC. Heracles threatens to put the captured boar into the sunken storage jar where Eurystheus has been hiding.*

V *The Cleansing of the Augeian Stables*

After absconding with Jason and the Argonauts on their quest for the Golden Fleece, Heracles returned to Tiryns for his fifth labour set by Eurystheus, angry at Heracles' recent disappearance. In a single day Heracles was to muck out the stables of the cattle of Augeias, King of Elis in the Peloponnese. Augeias' wealth depended on large herds of cattle, but there were so many of them that their dung lay too thickly on the fields for them to be tilled. Heracles demanded a payment of one-tenth of the cattle, and then proceeded to break a hole in the wall of the enclosure at a weak point shown to him by Athene, who was now his patron deity. He dug channels from the rivers Alpheius and Peneius and the area was flushed clean. Augeias refused to hand over the cattle and Heracles returned enraged to Tiryns where, to add salt to his wound, Eurystheus again refused to count it as a labour since Heracles had demanded a payment.

RIGHT Heracles and Athene cleaning the Augeian Stables; *metope sculpture from the Temple of Zeus at Olympia, c460 BC. Athene points to a weak spot in the river bank for Heracles to break and flood the land. This was the last of twelve sculpted metopes depicting the Labours; it was placed at the climax because the Labour was local to Olympia. Heracles' hair was left flat for paint and a metal helmet was attached to the holes in Athene's head. Athene's rather heavy drapery and relaxed standing pose are typical of Early Classical art.*

VI *The Stymphalian Birds*

Eurystheus sent Heracles back into Arcadia where a flock of birds, to escape local wolves, had settled on an island in the middle of Lake Stymphalus where they were now creating a nuisance to the local fishermen. The birds were hiding in the rushes when Heracles arrived armed with a pair of bronze castanets forged for him by Hephaestus. He climbed to the top of a mountain overlooking the lake and began to clash the castanets with all his might. Alarmed, the birds took flight in different directions; but Heracles had his catapult at the ready and many of them fell into the lake, others escaping never to return again.

VII *The Cretan Bull*

To date, all of Heracles labours had been in the Peloponnese on mainland Greece; there were no more monsters left for him to kill, no more fabulous creatures to bring home alive, and no more public nuisances to be cleaned up, so now Eurystheus asked his friends overseas if they had any similar problems. King Minos of Crete sent word that there was a wild bull roaming the fields outside of his palace at Knossos. In fact this was the bull that his wife Pasiphae had tricked into making love to her; she had been inspired with lust for the creature by Poseidon when Minos had refused to sacrifice this particularly handsome

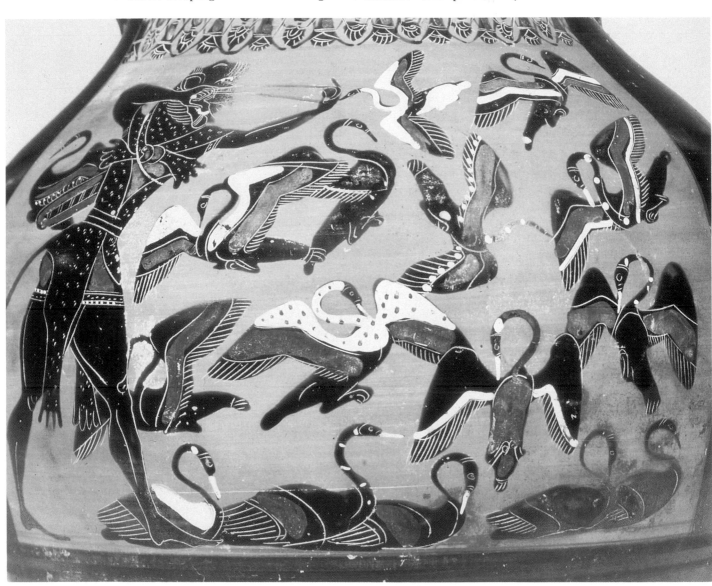

bull to the god. Every morning she would go out into the fields and attempt to seduce it, but to no avail – it was more interested in the dewy grass. The great craftsman Daedalus was asked to find a solution, and a few days later he presented her with a hollow wooden cow on wheels, which the next morning was pushed into the bull's field with a rather uncomfortable Pasiphae inside. It had the desired effect and Pasiphae's next baby had the head of a bull and was therefore named the Minotaur (Minos-Bull). Minos and Pasiphae were so embarrassed that they instructed Daedalus to construct the Labyrinth, a vast network of vaults beneath the palace, as a home for their curious son. Perhaps Minos wished to do away with his son's real father, and Heracles was the man to do it. The bull was brought back alive to Eurystheus, and one evening broke its tether and wandered off to Marathon ravaging the countryside until the arrival of Theseus.

VIII The Mares of Diomedes

Eurystheus heard that in Thrace there existed four horses, mares owned by the wicked king Diomedes, which lived on human flesh; with any luck they would be hungry when Heracles arrived to capture them for his eighth labour. Heracles made the long journey to Thrace by ship with Abderus, the young lover he had taken after the tragic loss of Hylas. Together they overpowered the grooms, but the alarm was raised and as they rushed the horses down to the waiting ship, Diomedes and his guard came in pursuit; Abderus went ahead with the mares while Heracles turned to kill Diomedes and sent his men running for cover. But when Heracles arrived at the beach he found that the four mares had proved too wild for his young friend and were finishing their tasty meal. Heracles drove them into the ship's hold and returned to bury what remained of Abderus, founding the city of Abdera on the burial mound in his memory. The mares were taken

to Tiryns, where Eurystheus freed them; on their way back to Thrace they were attacked by wolves on the slopes of Mount Olympus.

IX The Belt of Hippolyte

The next labour turned into a romantic adventure. Eurystheus' daughter Admete had as a child been told stories about the Amazons, a race of female warriors who lived beside the Black Sea on the River Thermodon. In her imagination she developed an admiration for their leader, Queen Hippolyte, who apparently wore a beautiful belt, studded with jewels. Admete suggested that Heracles should fetch it for her, and off he sailed with a crew of heroes. After a number of hostile encounters they arrived at last at Themiscyra, where the queen had her palace. Hippolyte was invited to a banquet on board during which she was struck by the charm of these handsome Greek heroes and wishing to ally herself to them, promised her belt to Heracles. Hera, annoyed at how smoothly Heracles was handling the task, disguised herself as an Amazon and informed the others that their queen was about to be kidnapped. The Amazons immediately attacked the ship and Heracles, thinking that Hippolyte had set him up, killed her and took the belt. Meanwhile, Prince Theseus, one of Heracles' companions, had fallen in love with Antiope, Hippolyte's sister, and he took her with him back to Athens.

X The Cattle of Geryon

Heracles delivered the belt to Eurystheus who gave it to his delighted daughter on her next birthday. There were three more labours left and Eurystheus was starting to panic, for he knew full well that if Heracles completed them he would claim his right to the throne at Tiryns. For the tenth labour therefore he decided that a really long journey to bring back the cattle of Geryon, a man with three heads, would exhaust

LEFT Heracles and the Stymphalian Birds; Athenian black-figure amphora, mid 6th century BC. Heracles uses a catapult to kill the birds, some of which can be seen falling from the sky while others continue to glide gracefully along on the lake. The painter has applied much purple and white to give colour to the exotic birds.

Heracles and that he would fall easy prey to one of the many monsters encountered on the way: there were plenty of them, for Heracles had never travelled westwards before. Geryon was King of Erytheia (Cadiz), and employed the herdsman Eurytion with his two-headed dog Orthus, son of Typhon, to guard his fine cattle. Heracles enjoyed the outward journey, killing all sorts of beasts on the way, and when he arrived at Oceanus on the edge of the world, he set up a pillar on either side of the straits which divide Africa and Europe as a monument to his great voyage. (They are still there, one now named the Rock of Gibraltar, the other the Jebel Musa in Morocco.) The Pillars of Heracles also served to keep the hideous sea-monsters of Oceanus out of the Mediterranean – they were too large to squeeze through.

Heracles leaned back against one

of the pillars, feeling tired and irritable and extremely thirsty. In his anger at the intense heat of the sun he rashly let loose an arrow in the direction of Helius, charioteer of the Sun. Luckily for him, Helius was in a good mood and admiring the daring of the hero, actually lent him his great golden drinking-cup for his journey to Erytheia, not to drink from, but to sail in. Heracles, club in hand to fend off the sharks, made good progress in the magic cup and soon arrived at Mount Abas where Geryon's cattle were grazing. Eurytion and Orthus ran at him, the hound's two heads barking and snarling; Heracles swung his club killing dog and herdsman with one stroke and quickly made off with the cattle. However Geryon had seen the sun bowl glittering in Oceanus and, troops at the ready, was soon pursuing Heracles. The cattle came to a halt at the River Anthemus, where Heracles turned and shot Geryon with three arrows, one for each head. Heracles decided that the strange boat was drawing too much attention and returned it with thanks to Helius, explaining that the cattle would spoil it.

Thus began his long journey eastwards back to Greece, and as Eurystheus had foreseen this proved to be dangerous, as so many coveted the cattle and lay in ambush for them. In Liguria (southern France) he was attacked and fell to his knees, badly wounded. Zeus came to his rescue by sprinkling rocks around Heracles to shield him; Heracles then hurled them at the retreating Ligurians. (The rocks still lie scattered to the west of Marseilles.)

Heracles then made his way down the west coast of Italy, where unbeknown to him the giant Cacus stole some of the cattle and hid them in his cave, which unfortunately for Cacus stood ahead beside the road (on the future site of Rome). As Heracles drove the noisy herd past the cave, the cattle hidden in the cave answered back revealing their hiding-place. Heracles was furious and killed the giant in a wrestling-bout, to the joy of the local people whose lives Cacus had made a misery. News of Heracles the Hero travelled ahead and everywhere in Italy he was met by joyful crowds, cheering and begging him to dispatch their own local nuisance down to Hades. In the lovely regions beneath the volcanic Mount Vesuvius, he founded a town called Herculaneum in his honour, which was destroyed by a violent volcanic eruption many, many centuries later.

Heracles eventually arrived at the tip of the Italian boot, where Hera caused the finest bull in the herd to break loose and swim the narrow straits to Sicily. Heracles asked the god Hephaestus, who had his forge beneath Mount Etna, to come and look after his cattle and swam off to find the bull. Heracles chased it across the island as far as its westernmost tip where the local king Eryx put it in with his own herds. The king wagered his lands against all of Geryon's cattle in a boxing match with the hero; though Eryx, famous for his boxing skills, put up an entertaining fight, Heracles son of Zeus was simply too powerful and soon Eryx lay dead. Mount Eryx remains as a memorial to the king.

XI The Apples of the Hesperides

When Hera married Zeus she had received many fine wedding presents from gods, giants and mortals alike, but her favourite gifts were some golden-apple trees created specially by Gaia, the earth mother. They grew somewhere in the west, but no one knew quite where. Heracles, for his eleventh labour was to bring back the valuable fruit to Eurystheus. Only Nereus, the Old Man of the Sea, knew where they grew and Heracles caught him napping on the sea-shore. Nereus turned himself into all sorts of slippery sea-creatures in an effort to escape, but Heracles' grip was too strong and soon the old man was telling where they could be found. It would not be easy for they were tended by the

Hesperides, Daughters of Evening, who lived near their father where Helius drives his chariot into Oceanus; and the tree on which the apples grew was entwined by a 100-headed snake called Ladon. Heracles had encountered monsters of this type before and did not foresee any difficulties. But, on the way, passing through the Caucasus mountains, he found the Titan, Prometheus, chained to a rock as eternal punishment for deceiving Zeus and stealing fire from the gods to give to men; Zeus' eagle was busy pecking his liver, which was renewed every day. Heracles decided to free the hero and shot the eagle. Prometheus in return advised Heracles to ask Atlas, the Titan whom Zeus had forced to carry the sky, to fetch the apples for him.

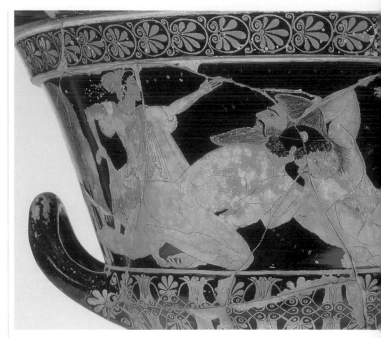

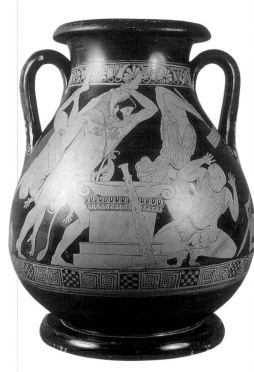

ABOVE Heracles and Busiris; Athenian red-figure pelike (wine-jar) by the Pan Painter, early 5th century BC. The hero is shown flinging King Busiris onto the altar where he himself was about to be sacrificed. The Egyptians are depicted with Negroid features.

Heracles passed through Arabia into Egypt, ruled at that time by the cruel king Busiris. At the start of his reign there had been terrible droughts which had led to famine. Busiris asked a seer from Greece for advice on what was to be done. The seer found that Zeus was angry with Busiris and was demanding the annual sacrifice of a foreigner in return for good harvests.

Busiris was a practical man and the unfortunate seer became the first of a line of foreign visitors to Egypt to be sacrificial victims. Heracles would make a fine sacrifice and he was bound and adorned and dragged to the altar where his father Zeus recognized him. Heracles broke his bonds in fury and proceeded to kill Busiris, together with his son and the priests, laying them on the altar as that year's sacrifice to Zeus.

From Egypt he made his way along the North African coast and came to Libya, where an eccentric young king called Antaeus ruled. Antaeus would challenge heroic visitors to wrestling matches and had never been beaten; and he always fought to the death. Heracles could not resist the challenge but found Antaeus' abilities to be more than he bargained for; every-time he pinned him to the earth to deliver the final blow Antaeus would throw Heracles off with replenished strength. Then he remembered what he had been told about Antaeus' parentage; his mother was Gaia and he was strong only so long as he kept in contact with her. Heracles changed his tactics by holding Antaeus from mother earth as often as he could, draining his strength and eventually killing him with a bear hug.

ABOVE Heracles fights Antaeus; Athenian red-figure calyx crater (wine mixing-bowl) signed by the painter Euphronios, late 6th century BC. The painter has used diluted 'paint' to depict the unkempt hair of the giant, who is in a highly contorted position while the hero's body is firm and true. The giant's right fingers are already limp as he begins to lose the fight.

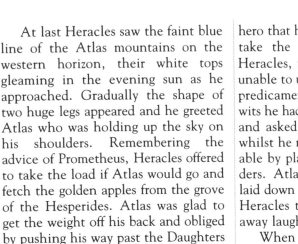

At last Heracles saw the faint blue line of the Atlas mountains on the western horizon, their white tops gleaming in the evening sun as he approached. Gradually the shape of two huge legs appeared and he greeted Atlas who was holding up the sky on his shoulders. Remembering the advice of Prometheus, Heracles offered to take the load if Atlas would go and fetch the golden apples from the grove of the Hesperides. Atlas was glad to get the weight off his back and obliged by pushing his way past the Daughters of Evening and strangling the hundred necks of Ladon. On his way back to the Atlas mountains, it dawned on him that he need never hold the sky again, and that Heracles could not come after him since he was unable to put down his load. He informed the hero that he felt like a walk and would take the apples to Tiryns himself. Heracles, for the first time in his life unable to use brute force to escape the predicament, had to rely on the few wits he had. He agreed to the proposal, and asked the Titan to hold the sky whilst he made himself more comfortable by placing a pillow on his shoulders. Atlas, who had no wits at all, laid down the apples and took the sky. Heracles took the apples and walked away laughing.

When he reached Tiryns, Eurystheus would not touch the apples, realizing that they were Hera's, so Heracles dedicated them at Athene's temple, since she had helped him to hold the sky. But she did not want them either and returned the sacred apples to the Hesperides.

RIGHT Athene, Heracles and Atlas with the apples of the Hesperides; *metope sculpture from the temple of Zeus at Olympia, c460 BC. The sculptor has depicted the hero supporting the heavens with Athene providing a helping hand; Atlas holds the apples. This was one of twelve metopes depicting the Labours which were positioned above the temple porches, six at each end.*

XII *Cerberus*

Eurystheus had to come up with something really lethal for the last labour. There were no more monsters or giants left on the earth; Heracles had annihilated them. 'Why not send him to the Underworld', thought Eurystheus, 'and let us see if he can bring Cerberus, the monstrous hound with three heads and a mane of snakes, up to the land of the living?' Cerberus undoubtedly held a grudge against Heracles for he had killed his brothers and sister: the Nemean Lion, the Hydra, and Orthus the dog.

To prepare himself for this twelfth and most difficult labour, Heracles was required to undergo ritual purification at Eleusis, where he was initiated into the secret Mysteries of Demeter and her daughter Persephone, goddess of the Underworld, to where Heracles now began his journey. Hermes was his guide into Hades' kingdom, and his patron deity Athene went with them as far as the gates near the birdless Lake Avernus. He tricked Cerberus by throwing him a cake soaked in opium, and while the dog snored Heracles pushed his way through the gates into the Underworld. As he became accustomed to the dark, he noticed the ghostly forms of the dead flitting away from him in fear; they appeared to be thirsty and Heracles killed one of the cattle of Hades and offered the blood to the shades as a drink. The cowherd protested and soon Heracles had cracked a couple of his ribs, only stopping when Persephone protested. In the mists he caught sight of two old friends, the heroes Theseus and Peirithous, who were seated in the two Chairs of Forgetfulness, Hades' punishment for attempting to carry off his wife Persephone. The chairs were of cold stone and anyone who sat in them turned to stone and became part of them, like enthroned statues of gods. He freed Theseus, but was afraid to untie Peirithous, the Lapith king, since the ground quaked as he approached him; Peirithous remains there to this day.

LEFT Heracles and Cerberus; *Athenian red-figure amphora by the Andokides Painter, late 6th century* BC. *The hero, holding a chain, approaches the dog with caution; Cerberus here has only two heads, each of which is surmounted by a cobra-like snake. Athene stands close by. The entrance to Hades is depicted as a temple porch.*

BELOW Heracles
brings Cerberus to
Eurystheus; *black-
figure* hydria (*water
jug*), *mid 6th century*
BC. *The hero and king
are both painted white,
a colour normally
reserved for women:
perhaps it suggests their
terror of the three-
headed dog, whom the
painter has depicted in
black, white and purple
with snakes on heads
and paws.*

Hades, seeing the havoc that the heroes were causing, agreed to Heracles' request to take Cerberus to Tiryns, but stipulated that Heracles must try to tame him without weapons, and return him as soon as the people of Tiryns had seen him. Heracles reluctantly agreed; he felt naked without his favourite weapons, but Hades was a god and he dutifully laid down his club, quiver and bow. Again he had to use his brain, and it occurred to him that dogs always attacked people who appeared to be frightened of them; so Heracles walked up casually to Cerberus and, patting him on his three heads, put a chain round each one and took him for a walk to the world above. Cerberus was delighted with this attention and barked with joy all the way to Tiryns. Eurystheus could not believe the advanced warnings of the hound's approach and stood on the ramparts laughing and calling the people of Tiryns to rejoice with him that Heracles was dead; there was a sudden terrifying growl behind him (Heracles had already trained Cerberus to attack cowards) and Eurystheus was back in his jar in a flash of Zeus' thunderbolt. Heracles was about to unchain his new pet, when Eurystheus reminded him that the labours were a sacred purification ceremony and that the gods would be angry if he let Cerberus loose. Heracles reluctantly agreed and took Cerberus back to the gates of Hades.

91

Heracles and Omphale

The twelve labours were over and Heracles remembered the words of the Pythia, who had promised that he would now achieve immortality. But such a promise does not bring happiness on earth, and for the rest of his life Heracles received more than his fair share of human misery. He could never find himself a new wife, since the story of his insane slaughter of Megara and their children was too well known. King Eurytus, who had once taught Heracles archery, refused the hand of his daughter and Heracles took some of his cattle instead. When accused of the theft by Iphitus, son of Eurytus, Heracles threw him off the roof of his palace. The gods punished him with illness; once again he went to Delphi for advice, but the Pythia, considering that he had not grown wiser after the labours, refused to answer him. In his anger he stormed off, taking the sacred tripod of Apollo with him. A fierce fight broke out between him and Apollo for the tripod, Heracles' first encounter with an Olympian; he was doing well and Zeus stopped the fight with a well-aimed thunderbolt and then ordered the Pythia to advise him of his new punishment. He was to be sold into slavery for three years, the proceeds going to the orphans of Iphitus.

At the slave market he was bought at a high price by Omphale, the beautiful Queen of Lydia. He cleared her land of giants and monsters, and some say also served her as a lover. Later authors even suggest that at Omphale's suggestion he wore womens' clothes and took to spinning and playing the lyre. However he spent his time in Lydia, he was still under the orders of the queen and after three years had become healthy again.

Heracles and Deianeira

After years spent avenging himself on former enemies, Heracles went to live in the court of King Oeneus of Calydon. He fell in love with princess Deianeira, but had to

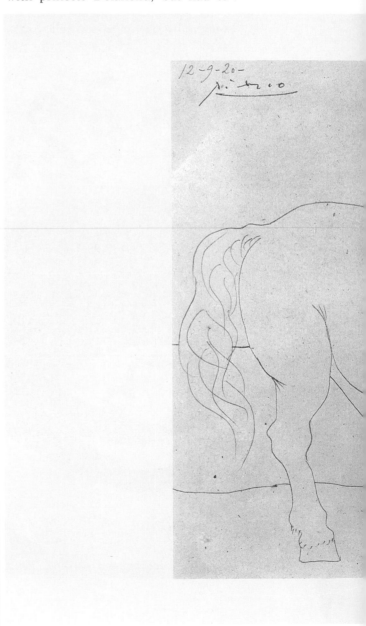

fight the local river-god Achelous for her hand; during the struggle Heracles broke off one of the god's horns which he later presented to the Hesperides, who filled it to the brim with fruit and named it the Cornucopia ('horn of plenty'). Heracles married Deianeira, but they were exiled from Calydon when Heracles, still not knowing his own strength, accidentally killed Oeneus's cup-bearer with a rap on the knuckles for spilling wine at a banquet. They made for Trachis and en route had to cross the wide river Evenus; Heracles was capable of swimming to avoid the high fees of the ferryman,

the Centaur Nessus, so he put Deianeira on the ferry whilst he himself swam. In the middle of the river he heard the cries of his wife whom Nessus was trying to rape. Heracles reached the opposite shore and killed the Centaur with an arrow, dipped in the poison of the Hydra. As he lay dying, Nessus, pretending remorse, told Deianeira that she should smear his blood on Heracles' clothes as a magical love potion which would make him always attracted by her. Fearing that one day Heracles would leave her for another woman she bottled the potion for future use.

LEFT *Pablo Picasso (1881–1973), Nessus and Dejanira (1920). Picasso carried Classical subjects into the present century. He was particularly interested in figures symbolic of the animal nature of man and made many sketches of the Minotaur. Here he depicts another classic half-man/half-beast, the Centaur Nessus, attempting the rape of Deianeira. The pencil drawing exhibits Picasso's mastery of foreshortening by means of single lines in the manner of Athenian red-figure vase-painters.*

Heracles was welcomed by the people of Trachis and helped them in many battles. He had one last vendetta against King Eurytus of Oechalia, who had once refused him his daughter Iole, as the prize of an archery contest won by Heracles. Eurytus was defeated and on his way back to Trachis with his new concubine Iole, Heracles stopped at Cape Cenaeum on the island of Euboea to build an altar to Zeus. He had no clean clothes for the sacrifice and sent his herald to Trachis to ask Deianeira for a fresh tunic. Deianeira heard from the herald Lichas that Heracles was in love with Iole, and,

remembering the Centaur's advice, smeared the tunic with the love potion. Heracles stood before the altar of Zeus in his new clothes. As he began the sacrifice his flesh began to burn; he ripped off the tunic, which took the flesh with it. In agony, he made his way back to Trachis where he found that Deianeira had committed suicide on learning that she had brought about the death of her husband.

The dying Heracles climbed Mount Oeta with his son Hyllus and ordered him to build a funeral pyre. The hero could not wait to die, but no one could bring themselves to light the pyre. At

last prince Philoctetes, who was passing by with his flocks, agreed to perform the sombre duty; Heracles rewarded him with his bow and arrows. A great crowd had gathered to witness the last moments of the great hero; they watched until the flames began to die away, and just as they were turning to depart a huge cloud rose above the pyre and there was a flash of lightning. The mists dispersed and no sign could be seen of the hero's body. Hyllus recalled the words of the Delphic oracle, related to his father many years earlier, that he would achieve immortality upon completion of the twelve labours.

Heracles was taken to Olympus by Athene and Hermes, where he was introduced to his divine father Zeus for the first time in his immortal life. He was reconciled with Hera, who gave him her daughter Hebe as a wife. Heracles continued to support his worldly allies against Eurystheus, who outlived Heracles on earth as king of Tiryns, and against the Trojans; Philoctetes was persuaded to join the Greeks on the Trojan plain where he killed Paris with the arrows of Heracles. Heracles remained hero of heroes for evermore.

LEFT The introduction of Heracles to Olympus; *Athenian black-figure wine-cup signed by the potter Phrynos, mid 6th century* BC. *This miniature scene was painted on the lip of the wine-cup. Athene, wearing her aegis (breastplate), introduces the hero to his father Zeus. Phrynos epoiesen chairemen ('Phrynos made this and sends his greetings') is signed beneath the scene. It exhibits the fine use of both brush and incising tool by a group of painters known as the 'Little Masters'. On the opposite side of the cup the painter depicted the birth of Athene, emphasizing the brother/sister relationship of goddess and hero.*

Archaeology and Temples

ABOVE *Mount Olympus, Greece; the snowy peak is nearly always obscured by clouds.*

Most Greek myths and legends had geographical locations in the real Greek world and covered the whole of the Mediterranean region. This does not necessarily mean that all Greeks had been to all places mentioned in the myths; the poets might have sometimes intentionally chosen unknown and therefore exotic settings for their stories which would have enhanced the magical and fantastic elements. (Shakespeare, for similar reasons, set many of his plays in real but exotic places where anything could happen.)

Perhaps the most famous location is Mount Olympus, the mythical home of the Olympian gods. Its snowy peaks are rarely visible, often shrouded in clouds which added to the sense of awe felt by the Greeks towards this most sacred of places. Archaeologists have recently discovered a ruined temple on the summit (at 9,186 ft/2,800 m), almost certainly dedicated to Zeus, the king of the Olympian gods. It is unlikely that this inhospitably sited temple was often used for worship, but remains of animal sacrifices, dedicatory inscriptions, and coins have been found in the recent excavations. It was linked by a sacred way to the city of Dion, down in the valley; here there were many rich temples dedicated to various Olympians. A statue of Dionysus, not one of the original twelve Olympians, and a temple of the Egyptian goddess Isis have also been found; the temple of Isis was built during the later Hellenistic period when the Greek world had expanded to embrace alien cultures and their religions. Dion was also the original location of the Olympic Games, organized in honour of Zeus, before they were transferred in the 8th century BC to Olympia in the Peloponnese. One tradition also places the home of the nine Muses, daughters of Zeus and Mnemosyne (Memory), on nearby Mount Pieria.

Other locations included well-known natural features of the landscape: Mount Etna in Sicily (which was full of Greek colonies) was for some the workshop of Hephaestus; others located the divine smith on the island of Lemnos, which had once been volcanic. Ancient writers of guide-books, such as Pausanias in the 2nd century AD pointed out other peculiar natural features such as boulders and chasms and explained them with myths.

Archaeologists have discovered clues as to the possible origins of certain myths. Romantic 19th-century travellers thought that they had discovered the Labyrinth of the Minotaur at Knossos in Crete; what they actually saw was the many-corridored prehistoric Minoan palace, but even this might have suggested the Labyrinth to the ancient poetic imagination.

Excavations at Troy have uncovered many stages of the ancient city; there is one particularly imposing city (Troy VI) which suffered great devastation in the 13th century BC (dated by pottery); this date approximately accords with the traditional dating of the fall of Troy in the early 12th century BC. It is highly probably that there was a siege of Troy by a confederacy of Greek nations, and that legendary figures like Achilles, Paris and Helen did exist; it would have been quite natural for the epic poets to exaggerate their strength and beauty for the amusement of their audiences. Other 'mythical' features such as monsters and divine epiphanies can be 'explained' in the same manner.

BELOW *Troy and the Trojan plain; the site of Homer's Troy was already a place of pilgrimage in antiquity. Great generals such as Alexander the Great, Julius and Augustus Caesar visited it to pay their respects to the* legendary heroes who *had fought and died there. The Greek forces were encamped on the plain beside the sea. The site now bears the trenches and mounds of Schliemann's 19th-century excavations.*

BOTTOM *The Trojan walls; these are the remains of later walls and a tower, but they give some idea of the size of the Homeric city, described in the Iliad as 'spacious' and 'surrounded by rings of stone'.*

97

RIGHT *The Athenian Acropolis ('Top of the City') was the main sanctuary of Classical Athens. It rises steeply from the plain and overlooks the whole of the city. This is a view of the Propylaea (entrance gates) with the little Temple of Athene Nike to the right. On the extreme right appears the top of the Parthenon.*

BELOW *The Parthenon or Temple of Athene Parthenos ('The Virgin') was designed by the architect Ictinus and built between 447 and 432 BC. Its partial survival is due to its conversion into a church and later a mosque. The many decorative sculptures have been destroyed or plundered over the years. Phidias's famous chryselephantine statue of Athene once stood inside.*

The Olympian gods were worshipped in walled sanctuaries. The most important building within the sanctuary was the temple, which was the home of the cult statue of the god; the temple was surrounded with a colonnade and was often decorated with sculptures referring to myths associated with the god (in much the same way as our churches have stained-glass windows illustrating bible stories). Before the temple, which faced the rising sun, was the altar where animal sacrifices were performed by priests or priestesses in front of worshippers who stood under colonnaded shelters called 'stoas'. Around the temple stood votive statues and other offerings dedicated by worshippers. Those who could not afford expensive bronze or marble statues would purchase terracotta images of the gods from booths outside the sanctuary; these were placed on the temple steps and later buried in sacred trenches which are today a rich source for our knowledge of Greek art and religion.

In the larger 'Panhellenic' sanctuaries such as that of Zeus at Olympia and Apollo at Delphi, city states would build their own treasuries along the sacred ways; these were often very fine buildings like miniature temples in which valuable offerings to the god were stored. Athletic competitions would be held every four years in honour of the gods; these sanctuaries therefore also contained stadia, gymnasia and statues of victorious athletes. A truce would be called throughout the Greek world whilst the games were being performed.

THESEUS

Aegeus, King of Athens, could not have children and sought the advice of the Delphic oracle. The Pythia's answer was that he should not loosen the spout of his wineskin until he arrived back at Athens. Aegeus did not understand the riddle and went to seek advice from his friend King Pittheus of Troezen before returning home. Pittheus grasped the Oracle's meaning immediately but pretended not to understand as he had hopes for his daughter Aethra; he plied Aegeus with wine and sent Aethra to sleep with him. The following morning the King of Athens left an ivory-handled sword and sandals beneath a huge rock in the palace yard, instructing the princess that if she bore a son who was able to lift the stone, she should send the boy to Athens with the sandals on his feet and the sword at his side. Little did he know that Poseidon came to Aethra on the same night.

The Labours of Theseus

Aethra did have a son and she named him Theseus. He grew into a strong and handsome young man, as might be expected, and believed his grandfather Pittheus who told him that his father was a god. Theseus loved to listen to the travelling poets with their stories of gods, giants and the heroes of Troy; but there was one hero who was still alive

and yet was already the subject of epic tales. His name was Heracles, and Theseus wished that he could one day be the subject of such grand stories. Theseus differed from Heracles in one respect: he was quick-witted and cultured, turning the brutish sport of wrestling into an athletic event for the highly skilled. One day Theseus lifted the stone, which had always been an obstacle to his gymnastic training, and Pittheus told him the story of Aegeus' sword and sandals. Theseus decided to set out for Athens, but refused to take the short sea crossing across the Saronic Gulf, preferring to travel on foot across the Isthmus which joins the Peloponnese to Attica. His excuse was that he suffered from seasickness, but really he wanted a chance to encounter the monsters and giants who, it was rumoured, lived beside this well-trodden route.

All travellers from southern to northern Greece were compelled to cross the narrow Isthmus; therefore, not surprisingly, many robbers dwelt in the area and made a living as highwaymen. One of the most notorious and feared was the giant Sinis, known as Pityocamptes; this name meant 'Pine-Bender' and referred to the manner in which Sinis would slay his victims. He used two methods: in one he would help the traveller to bend the top of a pine to the ground, at the last moment letting go so that the unwary stranger was shot high into the air; the second method was more terrible, Sinis would attach the victim's legs one to each of two bent pines and then release the trees, tearing the stranger in two. Theseus dispatched Sinis by the second method.

On his journey to Athens, Theseus also discovereed wild beasts and monsters which had been left alone by Heracles. One of these was a huge sow called Phaea by her parents Typhon and Echidna, children of Titans; the beast was terrorizing the farms around Crommyon, but Theseus killed her with a single blow. Already Theseus was becoming renowned in Greece, and it was not long before rumours of this new hero had reached King Aegeus at Athens.

Beside the Isthmus are rocks and cliffs known as the Rocks of Sciron. Passing travellers would be welcomed by Sciron, offered a drink and told to put their feet up. After this refreshment he would ask them to wash his feet in return; but while they were drying his feet he would suddenly kick them unsuspecting over the precipice to fall into the jaws of a giant turtle waiting at the foot of the cliffs. Theseus accepted the hospitality, and returned the favour by washing Sciron's feet, considering this good behaviour for a royal prince. He was too skilled in the art of wrestling for the sudden kick to catch him off his guard and, taking hold of the robber's ankles, hurled him over his shoulders to become the turtle's last meal.

Theseus continued on his way to Athens and soon had reached Eleusis. Here he was welcomed by King Cercyon, who demanded a wrestling bout with the stranger. The king's style of fighting was barbaric and he had already killed a number of passing travellers by sheer brute force. In the palace at Troezen, Theseus had received a fine education in both fighting and the arts, and had developed rules and skills for the generally violent physical activities hoping to encourage sportsmanship among otherwise cultured peoples. Here at Eleusis was his chance to set an example; barbaric Cercyon smashed and grabbed, but Theseus used his skills and swift footwork to avoid and parry the blows, to the delight and applause of onlookers. Cercyon died of sheer exhaustion. Theseus set up a training school at Eleusis where athletes would be taught to box and wrestle in a civilized manner.

Theseus stayed the night just outside Eleusis at the inn of Damastes, whose nickname Procrustes ('Stretcher') was only understood when he showed his guests to their bedrooms. Wanting the tall ones to be comfortable, he made sure that their beds fitted exactly by sawing off any limbs

LEFT The Labours of Theseus; *Athenian red-figure wine-cup, 5th century* BC. *In the centre Theseus kills the Minotaur and pulls the body outside the Labyrinth. Around the outside of the cup the hero punishes Sinis (tied to the tree), Sciron (note the turtle) and Procrustes (having his legs removed to fit the bed) and captures the Bull of Marathon.*

which hung over the end of the bed. The short guests would have weights attached to their feet until they also fitted their beds exactly. Theseus put an end to the innkeeper's mad tricks by returning his gruesome hospitality.

On the following morning Theseus at last received his first glimpse of his destination; the palace and shrines on the Acropolis, the precipitous limestone hill which dominates the Athenian plain, were grander than any he had seen. As he was passing by the wayside Temple of Apollo Delphinius, some workmen on the roof of the temple jeered and whistled, thinking from his appearance that he was a young girl. Theseus was always well dressed as a civilized prince should be but he realised that his ankle-length gown was the fashion for Athenian women and that men wore a short tunic. However, he lost his temper and hurled two oxen from a passing cart up above the roof of the temple to the astonishment of the workmen.

King Aegeus had stopped at Corinth on his way back to Athens from Troezen; at the royal palace he had met the oriental princess Medea, who had been spurned by her husband Jason when he took a new wife at Corinth. Medea, famous for her witchcraft, had avenged herself on Jason by killing his new bride with a burning cloak, as well as murdering her two sons by him. She had flown to Athens in a dragon-drawn chariot, the gift of her grandfather Helius, and promised to bear Aegeus children if he would protect her at Athens. They had a son called Medus, whom Medea wished to see made king of Athens. Only she recognized Theseus as the boy whom Aegeus had once told her would one day come to Athens as the royal heir, but she kept this knowledge to herself. Aegeus held a splendid banquet for the new hero, whose exploits along the road from Troezen were already the subject of Athenian drinking songs; Theseus had become as renowned a hero as Heracles.

Medea, however, persuaded Aegeus that Theseus was actually an enemy who had come to overthrow the king; they sent him off to kill the bull of Marathon, which Heracles had brought from Crete years earlier as one of his labours. Medea and Aegeus knew that Theseus would be killed, and that being a hero he could not refuse the challenge. Theseus captured the bull on the plains of Marathon and triumphantly brought it back alive to prove his heroism to the people of Athens; he presented it to Aegeus for sacrifice. That evening at a celebratory banquet Medea slipped poison in the hero's cup; just as he was about to drink, Aegeus noticed the ivory-handled sword hanging at Theseus's side and knocked the poisoned cup from his hands. Theseus was welcomed as the new prince of Athens and the people rejoiced that such a brave and handsome hero would one day be king.

Theseus and the Minotaur

Later that year Theseus learnt of a disturbing event that took place every nine years at Athens. A generation earlier King Minos of Crete had attacked Athens and demanded tribute of seven boys and seven girls, who were to be sent to Crete as a nine-yearly feast for the Minotaur, his monstrous son born from the union of his queen, Pasiphae, and the bull of Marathon when it had lived on Crete; it had a bull's head and a man's body and represented to the Athenians all the uncontrolled lusts and animal qualities of uncivilized barbarians. Theseus asked Aegeus why his own name was not placed in the jar for the lottery which decided which unlucky children were to be sent to Crete; Aegeus laughed and answered that a prince did not count as a tribute. Theseus demanded that he should replace one of the chosen boys – he determined to slay the Minotaur.

The seven boys and seven girls of Athens sailed out from Piraeus, the port of Athens, in the black-sailed ship of Minos himself. Aegeus sadly told the captain to hoist a white sail on the return trip if Theseus was

RIGHT Theseus and Athene in the underwater palace of Amphitrite; *Athenian red-figure wine-cup, signed by Euphronios as potter and Onesimos as painter; early 5th century BC. The underwater scene with swimming dolphins and a Triton supporting Theseus' feet would have been enhanced by the sea of wine that covered it. The drapery is depicted swaying in the sea-currents. Euphronios epoiesen ('Euphronios made this') is signed to the left of the young Theseus. On the cup exterior were painted further heroic exploits of Theseus.*

successful, so that preparations could be made for the triumphant home-coming. On the sea-journey to Crete Theseus, hearing the cries of one of the seven girls whom the lusty Minos was pestering, challenged him to a show of strength. Minos called on his father Zeus to hurl a thunderbolt into the sea as proof of his own divine parentage; a flash of lightning duly appeared, and Minos arrogantly threw his gold ring into the sea, challenging Theseus to prove that his father was Poseidon by retrieving it. Theseus dived without hesitation and had soon reached his father's palace; he was welcomed by Amphitrite, the lovely wife of Poseidon, who not only handed him Minos's ring, but also placed on his brow a beautiful wreath of roses and wrapped him in a purple cloak. Theseus was soon standing on deck miraculously dry. The Nereids rode the waves beside the ship and the Athenian children joined them in their songs of praise; Minos was greatly disturbed and left the girls alone for the rest of the journey.

LEFT Theseus fighting
the Minotaur;
Athenian red-figure
stamnos (wine mixing-
jar) by the Kleophrades
Painter, early 5th
century BC. The hero's
pony-tailed hair reflects
the new 5th-century
fashion for short or tied
hair. Diluted 'paint'
depicts blood on the
Minotaur, who holds a
stone as a weapon.
Theseus' hat and
scabbard hang on the
wall.

RIGHT Theseus and
the Minotaur; Roman
wall-painting from a
Pompeian house, 1st
century AD. The
Minotaur lies dead in
the entrance to the
Labyrinth. The hero is
praised by both children
and adults.

RIGHT Dionysus and
Ariadne; red-figure
wine-cup, 5th
century BC. The
drunken Dionysus,
wearing an ivy wreath,
holds a lyre and is
supported by his mortal
lover Ariadne. Eros,
depicted in the 5th
century BC as an
adolescent youth with
long hair and wings,
plays a tambourine.
The vine leaves and
grapes which decorate
the top of the bowl
would be reflected in
the wine.

On Crete, as was the custom on the night before feeding them to the Minotaur, Minos entertained his young guests at his palace at Knossos. At the banquet Princess Ariadne fell in love with Theseus and offered to help if he took her back to Athens with him. The Minotaur lived in a maze beneath the palace called the Labyrinth; Ariadne gave Theseus a plan of the Labyrinth which its architect, the famous craftsman Daedalus, had given her to spite King Minos. The next morning the young Athenians were thrown into the maze; Ariadne gave Theseus a ball of string and attached one end of it to the Labyrinth's exit. Theseus stepped into the darkness, unravelling the twine as he stepped over the skeletons of earlier victims. He heard the bellowings of the monster in the distance and made his way towards them; at last he found the Minotaur in a great hall at the centre of the maze about to strangle one of the children. Theseus used his wrestling skills, but finding that they were ineffective against the beast, killed it with a well-aimed blow of his fist. He gathered the Athenians together and, guided by the twine, was soon back in the open air. Ariadne had prepared the ship for sailing and soon they were safely on their way towards Athens. There was great rejoicing on board that night.

The ship stopped for water at the island of Dia (Naxos); where Theseus cruelly abandoned Ariadne on the beach. She watched his ship disappear over the horizon and, greatly distressed, prepared to hang herself; but as she placed the noose around her neck she heard distant music and singing. Coming towards her along the beach was a group of Maenads following a beautiful youth with ivy-strewn hair and a thyrsos in his hand. She knew immediately that this was the god Dionysus and their love lasted for many years. When she died Dionysus placed among the stars the crown which he had given her at their wedding, the constellation Corona Borealis.

Perhaps Theseus' callous behaviour was repaid: as the ship approached Athens, the captain, caught up in the excitement of the rejoicing passengers, had forgotten to hoist the white sail. King Aegeus was standing on the edge of the Acropolis when he saw the mournful sign of the black sail; thinking his son dead, he jumped to his death.

Theseus, King of Athens

Theseus, after mourning his father, received a splendid coronation and set about improving the kingdom of Athens. He persuaded the outlying towns of Athens, the Demes, to support an Athenian commonwealth, and reduced his own royal powers; an early step towards democracy, which later took him as its hero.

Heracles honoured the new king by inviting him on an expedition, his ninth labour, to the Black Sea where the Amazons lived; his task was to bring back the belt of Queen Hippolyte as a gift for Eurystheus' daughter. Hippolyte and her relatives were invited to a banquet on board the Greek ship; Theseus fell in love with Antiope, sister to the queen, and took her back to Athens where they married and had a son called Hippolytus. Antiope was killed when an army of Amazons marched against Athens in an unsuccessful attempt to win her back.

Theseus thought it would be sensible to form a political alliance with Crete and arranged to marry Minos's daughter Phaedra – the abandonment of her sister Ariadne had apparently been forgotten. Demophon and Acamas were their two sons and became heirs to the Athenian throne; Hippolytus had already been sent to Troezen where he became heir to his great-grandfather Pittheus.

During an attempted political coup, Pallas, the half-brother of Aegeus, and his fifty sons were killed by Theseus; the oracle instructed Theseus to go into exile for one year as purification for the spilling of family blood. He decided to spend the year at Troezen. Theseus and his court were welcomed at Troezen by Hippolytus. When Phaedra saw him she shuddered as she recognized the beautiful young man she had once seen at an initiation ceremony to the goddess Demeter at Eleusis. Phaedra's love for this handsome stranger had been inspired by Aphrodite and Phaedra had built a shrine to the goddess on the corner of the Acropolis; on a clear day she could see Troezen, where she knew he lived, but until the day she arrived there with her husband she was unaware that this was the son of Theseus by another woman. Hippolytus himself had become a fine hunter and had vowed his chastity to the virgin goddess of the chase, Artemis.

BELOW *Peter Paul Rubens (1577–1640), Battle of the Amazons. Rubens represents a scene popular in Classical art: Greek males fighting the Amazon warriors. The Greeks used the subject to demonstrate the triumph of civilized patriarchal society over barbarian societies with feminine characteristics. The wives of Greek citizens lived in purdah.*

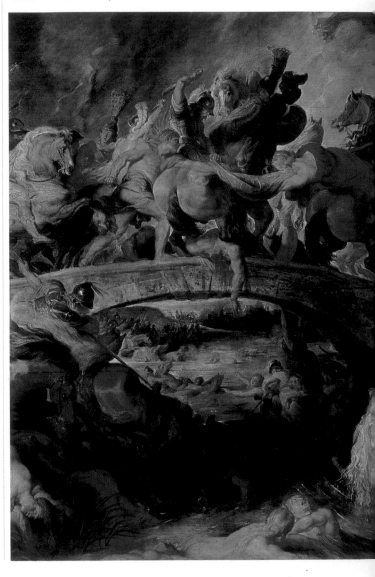

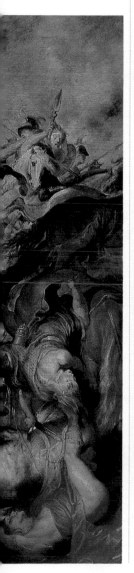

RIGHT *Pierre-Auguste Renoir (1841–1919), Diana (1867). Renoir has painted the virgin Artemis (Diana) as a contemporary beauty seated in a sunny French landscape. She wields a very unclassical longbow with which she has just killed a deer.*

While Theseus was away at Delphi Phaedra found herself wasting away with unrequited love for her stepson. Her nurse secretly informed Hippolytus of Phaedra's feelings, but he was disgusted. Phaedra, driven to despair, committed suicide after writing a letter in which she spitefully informed Theseus that Hippolytus had raped her. Theseus returned and read the letter; refusing to believe his son's innocence, he called on his father Poseidon to destroy him. One day Hippolytus was riding his chariot along the beach when a huge bull rose from the sea and terrified the prince's horses; Hippolytus became entangled in the reins and was dragged over the rocks to his death. Theseus later learnt the truth from the priestess of Artemis; Aphrodite had arranged the tragedy because Hippolytus had refused to worship her, preferring chaste Artemis.

The Lapith King Peirithous invited Theseus to his marriage with Hippodameia. He also invited the Centaurs, who have the upper half of men but from the waist downwards are all horse. These semi-wild creatures had never drunk wine before and at the first taste their animal natures took control and they tried to rape the women. A fight ensued between Lapith and Centaur, and, with Theseus leading them, the Lapiths won.

After the deaths of Hippodameia and Phaedra, Peirithous and Theseus decided that they must find divine wives. Theseus forcibly abducted Helen, born from the egg of Zeus after he made love to Leda as a swan; but her heroic brothers, the Dioscuri, Castor and Polydeuces, won her back only to find her abducted again by Paris of Troy. Perithous decided to try to win Persephone from Hades; the two heroes were captured and imprisoned on the two chairs of Lethe (Forgetfulness), to make them forget their sacrilegious act. Heracles freed Theseus when he came on his last labour to capture the guard dog Cerberus.

Theseus, unlike Heracles, died an ignominious mortal death. He slipped over a cliff on the island of Scyros, where he had come to reclaim some lands which had once belonged to his grandfather; some say he was pushed. As he fell towards the rocks below, Theseus remembered the similar fates of the robber Sciron, of his beloved father Aegeus, and of his son Hippolytus.

LEFT Lapith fighting Centaur; *metope sculpture from the Parthenon, Athens, 447–432 BC. The Parthenon's exterior Doric frieze was decorated with 92 sculpted metopes. Four subjects were represented, one for each side of the temple: Greeks fighting Trojans; Greeks fighting Amazons; gods fighting giants and Lapiths fighting Centaurs. The subjects symbolized the victory of the civilized Greeks over the Persians earlier in the century. Here the sculptor produces a circular tension between the man and half-beast, while the spread drapery makes an effective backdrop.*

BELOW Theseus and Peirithous in the Underworld; *Athenian red-figure calyx-crater (wine-mixing jar) by the Niobid Painter, mid 5th century BC. The subject is disputed, but might well depict the two heroes seated in Hades with Heracles and Athene standing above them. The painter has attempted (for the first time in vase-painting) to convey an impression of depth by placing the figures on different levels; the rocky landscape is drawn in thin white lines.*

PERSEUS

Acrisius, the King of Argos, had been told by an oracle that he would one day be killed by a grandson. Therefore, he arranged for his daughter Danae to be locked in a cell of bronze until she was too old to have children; one day however he learnt that she had become miraculously pregnant. Zeus had plans for the future of Argos and had come to her one night through an air vent in the roof of the cell as a beautiful shower of gold dust. She bore a son and named him Perseus, but Acrisius had them thrown into the sea in a wooden chest. They were washed up on the island of Seriphos, where a friendly fisherman named Dictys gave them shelter. When Perseus reached manhood, Danae told him who his father was.

Perseus and Medusa

Dictys' lusty brother Polydectes was the King of Seriphos. He wanted to marry Danae but Perseus defended his unwilling mother. Angry at this rebuttal, Polydectes demanded horses from all the islanders as a gift to Hippodameia, daughter of King Oenomaus of Pisa, whom he now wished to marry. Perseus had no horses but said that he would provide anything else that the king might suggest, even the head of the Gorgon Medusa. Polydectes knew that no man had ever returned from visiting the Gorgons and confidently sent Perseus off to fulfil his rash promise.

Zeus sent Athene to give help and advice to his son. She directed him to a cave in Libya, where three hags called the Graeae dwelt; they would tell him where to find certain nymphs who were preparing special weapons to defeat the Gorgons. The Graeae, sisters of the Gorgons, refused to help Perseus. They possessed only one eye and one tooth between them and as one was passing the eye to the other

LEFT *Titian (c1487–1576), Danae and the Shower of Gold, (1554). The painting was commissioned as one of a number of erotic Classical subjects for Philip II of Spain. The painting depicts Danae not in the bronze prison of the Classical myth but in a luxurious bedroom complete with pet dog and a servant who tries to gather the gold in her apron. Titian described the painting as 'poesie' – a poetic fantasy of the myth.*

to look at the stranger, Perseus grabbed it and refused to return it unless they told him the whereabouts of the nymphs. He found them and they presented him with the weapons: a pouch in which to place Medusa's severed head; a pair of winged sandals to make a quick escape from her two immortal sisters, Stheno and Euryale, who had golden wings and hands of bronze; and a magical cap to make him invisible to perform the task. Hermes provided a sickle of sharpened adamant and helped him to polish his bronze shield until it shone like a mirror; this would be useful in enabling him to look at the reflected image of the Gorgons, who turned all who looked at them to stone.

Perseus recognized the approach to the Gorgons' lair by the petrified images of men and women who had caught sight of them; the sisters had placed them like marble statues on either side of the path. Invisible in his magic cap, Perseus approached Medusa, watching her reflection carefully in his shield. She was hideous, with snakes instead of hair and a huge red tongue hanging from her mouth between tusks. Perseus decapitated her with one swing of the sickle and, placing the head in the pouch, flew away swiftly in his winged sandals; Stheno and Euryale could not keep up with him and finally returned to mourn their dead sister.

On the way home Perseus stopped for the night in the land of the Hesperides. Atlas, who stood guard over their garden which contained the magic apples of Hera, had been told that one day a son of Zeus would come and steal them. He therefore tried to kill Perseus, who produced the Gorgon's head and turned the Titan into a high peak, Mount Atlas.

Perseus and Andromeda

As Perseus flew along the coast of Ethiopia he spied far below a naked girl chained to a rock by the sea. He flew nearer and heard her crying for help; two sad figures, her

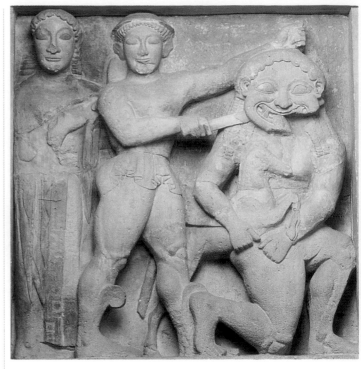

parents King Cepheus and Queen Cassiopeia, were standing on the cliff and Perseus learnt from them what was happening: Cassiopeia had vainly boasted that her daughter was prettier than the Nereids; they had complained to Poseidon who had sent a sea-monster to terrorize Ethiopia. An oracle had told Cepheus that the monster would leave them alone only if he were to offer it his daughter Andromeda. Perseus promised to destroy the monster if the king and queen would allow him to marry Andromeda; at that moment the creature raised its long neck above the waves and dived, heading underwater for Andromeda's rock. Cepheus agreed and Perseus slew the monster with his sickle; it lay dead on the beach beneath the lovely Andromeda whom he unchained and delivered back to her parents. There was a celebratory banquet at the palace that night and Cepheus announced his daughter's marriage to the new hero, forgetting that he had already promised her to his brother Phineus. A fight started and Perseus, realizing that he was far outnumbered by Phineus and his troops, petrified them with the head of Medusa.

Perseus sailed to Seriphos with

LEFT *Perseus and
Medusa; limestone
metope sculpture from
a Greek temple at
Selinus, Sicily, mid 6th
century* BC. *The
winged horse Pegasus
appears beside his
mother Medusa, while
Athene stands to the
left. The profile bodies
with frontal 'smiling'
faces are typical of
Archaic art.*

Andromeda and discovered on arrival that King Polydectes was still pursuing his mother Danae. Leaving Danae and Andromeda with Dictys, he went to the royal court and announced that he had returned with the gift for Hippodameia; out of its pouch came Medusa's head and all were turned to stone. He returned the magic cap, winged sandals and sickle to Hermes who took them back to the African nymphs; the head of Medusa was dedicated to Athene, who attached it to her aegis (breastplate) as a formidable weapon. Perseus decided to return to his birthplace at Argos and claim his inheritance from King Acrisius.

Though Perseus was prepared to forgive his past behaviour, Acrisius fled to King Teutamides, remembering the prophetic words of the oracle. Perseus left Danae and Andromeda at Argos and travelled to Larisa, where Teutamides was holding funeral games

in honour of his father. Perseus could not see Acrisius among the crowds of spectators and decided to wait until the evening banquet; in the meantime he would compete in the games and introduced an event of his own called 'throwing the discus'. He took up the metal disk and hurled it into the open spaces of the stadium; but the wind suddenly diverted it and the discus landed in the crowd, killing Acrisius and thus fulfilling the prophecy.

Perseus returned to his mother and wife at Argos, but realized that the gods would consider it wrong for him to rule over the city of the man he had killed. He therefore exchanged Argos with nearby Tiryns where he ruled for many years, founding several other cities in the Argolid including Mycenae. Andromeda bore him several children and his grandson Eurystheus became the last of the Perseid dynasty at Argos. Perseus died a natural death.

LEFT *Sir Edward Coley
Burne-Jones (1833–
98),* The Doom
Fulfilled. *Burne-Jones
brings a Romantic
medieval atmosphere to
the myth of Perseus'
rescue of Princess
Andromeda. The
hero's armour and
winged greaves are
distinctly exotic whilst
the hair of Medusa's
head spills from his
shoulder-bag.
Andromeda is free of
her chains but awaits
the outcome of the
fight.*

The Greek Poets

RIGHT *Rhapsode reciting; Athenian red-figure amphora by the Kleophrades Painter, early 5th century BC. The painter has inscribed the start of an epic poem emerging from the poet's mouth: 'As once in Tiryns . . .'. Tiryns was a powerful Greek Mycenaean palace at the time of the Trojan war.*

In prehistoric Greece the myths were transmitted orally by professional poets called 'rhapsodes'. Their patrons were the Greek-speaking kings and aristocrats who governed relatively small areas of the Mediterranean. The rhapsodes would travel from court to court, often staying for several days to recite lengthy epic poems from memory: Mnemosyne (Memory) was the mother of the Muses who inspired poets. These epics were first recorded by poets such as Homer when writing was introduced in the 8th century BC. Their subjects concerned the origins of the gods and giants as well as legends of wars fought by their ancestors centuries ago. The most popular saga was the siege of Troy by the Greeks and their heroic adventures both before and after the siege. Relying on memory and wishing to hold the attention of their audiences, who would normally be wining and dining, the rhapsodes decorated their stories with superhuman activities and encounters with gods and monsters. Their language was suitably high-flown and the poems were sung in strict metre often to musical accompaniment.

Here is a description of the Greek hero Achilles from Homer's *Iliad*, translated by Alexander Pope in 1715:

> The Hero rose;
> Her aegis Pallas o'er his shoulders throws;
> Around his brows a golden cloud she spread;
> A stream of glory flamed above his head.
> As when from some beleaguered town arise
> The smokes high-curling to the shaded skies
> (seen from some island, o'er the main afar,
> When men distressed hang out the sign of war),
> Soon as the Sun in ocean hides his rays,
> Thick on the hills the flaming beacons ablaze;
> With long-projected beams the seas are bright,
> And heaven's high arch reflects the ruddy light;
> So from Achilles' head the splendours rise,
> Reflecting blaze on blaze against the skies.

There were also the lyric poets, who composed short poems for the symposia, intimate drinking parties held among a few close friends; they sung in short verses and accompanied themselves on the lyre – hence the name 'lyric'. Their subject matter was more personal than epic, dealing with apparently spontaneous outpourings of love, political satire and other themes relating to the lie of the *polis* (city-state). One of the earliest surviving lyric poets is

Sappho of Lesbos (c620–c550 BC), who recited her poems at symposia which seem to have been attended mainly by women.

In the following poem Sappho employs the myth of Helen to show the power of Aphrodite in influencing feelings of love. Sappho subverts the male values of war, preferring unadorned natural female beauty to the artificial glamour of armed warriors.

What is the most beautiful sight on this black earth?
Some will answer cavalry, or infantry, or warships;
But the woman I most love
Is lovelier than all these.

My answer is easily explained,
For Helen, more beautiful than all on earth,
Left doting parents, princely husband, child
To cross the sea for Troy: love at first sight.

After all, teenage brides have fragile hearts,
Which filled with passions newly poured
Are readily persuaded
By Aphrodite, Cypriot Queen.

I am no different when I think of Anaktoria
As she left me: at her sensual walk and glimmering
    pearly face
I would prefer to gaze
than richly decorated Lydian chariots filled with
    weapons.

(Translated by David Bellingham)

Choral odes were composed by lyric poets for more public occasions, such as weddings and religious festivals. These would include a colourful mixture of song and dance delivered by a chorus. They would employ myths to honour the patron, which might be a newly wed couple, a victor in the athletic games, or the *polis* itself. Bacchylides, writing in the 5th century BC, composed a choral hymn of praise to the hero Theseus, to be performed at a festival in honour of Apollo on his sacred island of Delos; it was sung by the poet's fellow islanders from Keos. King Minos of Crete, who is bringing Theseus and other young Athenian to offer as a sacrifice to the Minotaur, sends Theseus into the sea to fetch a golden ring to prove his heroism and divine favour. At the end of the poem Theseus emerges

ABOVE Symposium and Gorgon's head; Athenian black-figure wine-cup, mid 6th century BC. The drinkers hold similar wine-cups and one of them plays the aulos (double-pipe); a naked boy offers more wine. The Gorgon's head would appear as the drinker finished his wine.

from the sea triumphantly wearing a wreath given to him
by the sea-goddess Amphitrite; the mythical narrative ends
with songs of praise which return us to the present
moment and the festival of Apollo:

He came to the surface beside the narrow ship's stern;
What a shock for the King of the armies of Knossos,
To see him standing there all dry.
All were amazed at the gleaming godly gifts he wore
And Nereids cried in delight from their glittering
   thrones
Riding the sea which echoed with their laughter.
The young Athenians praised him with songs of love.
Lord of Delos, your soul moved by our Kean voices,
Now send us your blessings from the heavens above.

(Trans. David Bellingham)

In the 5th century BC Athens was at the centre of
Greek culture, attracting the best artists and writers with
wealthy patronage. The most influential poetic form at
this time was tragedy. Annual festivals to Dionysus cul-
minated in dramatic competitions in the large open-air
theatre of Dionysus on the slopes of the Acropolis. These
plays took the form of trilogies performed in one day with a
'satyr play' in the evening to lighten the mood. Their subjects were drawn from mythology, but they usually dealt
with matters of contemporary relevance: in the *Oresteia*
trilogy by Aeschylus we are taken from the aftermath of
the Trojan wars in the first two plays to contemporary
Athens in the final play where we witness the first trial by
jury under the new democracy. Other plays, such as
Euripides' *Trojan Women* (415 BC), deal with Greek attitudes towards women; Andromache speaks:

The woman whom people really gossip about
Is the one who refuses to remain housebound.
I would love to have gone out, but dutifully
Stayed at home; and I did not answer back
Like some women do. My mind was sound enough
And taught me how to behave as nature intended.
What more did I need?
I would speak only when spoken to
And appear meek and mild before my husband.
I knew what was expected of me
And when to let him have his own way.

(Translated by David Bellingham)

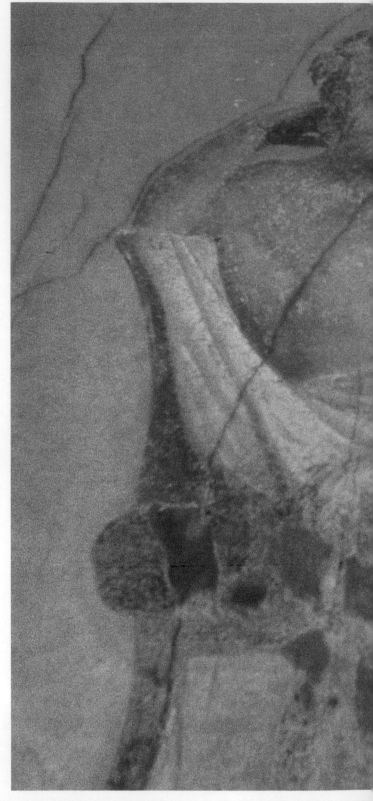

These early poetic uses of myth continued into the Hellenistic and Roman periods, but there are changes of emphasis. Greek poetry and art continued to be signs of high cultural attainment for Hellenistic kings and Roman emperors. Poets became increasingly learned in their use of myth and expected similar levels of understanding in their audiences. Callimachos, librarian at Alexandria in Egypt in the 3rd century BC, wrote for a royal patron and his court. An increasing tendency among poets in the Hellenistic period was to dwell on the minor details and previously unimportant episodes of the myths: the heroes and heroines became more human and Callimachos responded to a desire among the sophisticated urban elite for romantic images of country peasants. In the poem 'Hecale', Theseus is on his way to fight the bull of Marathon and seeks shelter from a storm in an old woman's cottage:

Theseus threw off his soaking clothes
And putting on a ragged tunic that she had laid out on
   the bed
Made himself at home on her humble couch.
She meanwhile had built a fire from wood stored long
   ago
And brought him a cauldron of boiling water;
'Have you a bowl for me to soak my feet in?', asked
   Theseus.
When he had finished she emptied the bowl and brought
   him
Another cup of wine and water.
She brought him black and green olives, which she had
   gathered wild
In the Autumn, now swimming in brine;
From a pipkin she served him loaves,
And while Theseus ate the ploughman's lunch,
Hecale told him the story of her life
For she had once come from a wealthy family . . .

(Translated by David Bellingham)

LEFT The poet
Menander; *Roman
wall-painting from the
House of the Menander,
Pompeii, 1st century
AD. Menander was a
4th-century BC writer
of Greek comedy. He is
shown here reading
from a papyrus scroll,
the normal medium for
published poetry.*

ORIENTAL MYTHOLOGY

120

Chinese Mythology

The Chinese people have never demanded a clear
separation of the worlds of myth and reality – indeed,
they are so closely bound up that it is hard to say where
one begins and the other ends. Historical figures are
made into gods and myths are recounted as history.
Even in revolutionary China, the same processes could
be seen at work: Chairman Mao, in the heyday of the
Cultural Revolution (1968–78), was often seen as the
all-powerful god responsible for all good things that
happen. When an airline hostess can offer the
explanation that 'there is no need to wear a safety belt,
because Mao, the Great Helmsman, is in charge', the
feeling is that superhuman characters with fantastic
powers, like those that inhabited the ancient texts, are
alive and well in the 20th century.

*An apsara, a heavenly being, in the form of a musician flying on a cloud; this grey
limestone carving dates from the early 6th century and comes from the Buddhist cave
temples at Longmen, Henan province.*

Confusing though the tendency to intertwine fact and fantasy may be for the westerner, it indicates the power and importance of 'mythology' in the Chinese tradition. Chinese people chart their history in an unbroken line back through the dynasties to the world of Nugua and Fuxi, moving seamlessly from a historical to a mythical time-scale. The earliest archaeological evidence supports the existence of the Shang people in the 12th century BC in the basin of the Yellow River, 'the cradle of Chinese civilization', at about the same time as the beginning of Greek culture. As in Greece, by the 4th century BC, China had a society that was highly developed, and many of the distinguishing features of Chinese life then, have been passed down in recognizable form to the 20th century. The achievement of such a striking degree of stability in their social system is one of the Chinese people's most remarkable accomplishments.

The most important means that China used to secure the survival of its social system was its ability to modify and absorb foreign influences. Those who tried to conquer found themselves in confrontation with a society more complex and sophisticated than their own, and even when successful in their military endeavour, usually ended by adopting Chinese practices and political structures. This was the case when the nomadic Manchu tribes conquered China from the north and established the Qing dynasty in the 17th century. But the most significant influence on Chinese development to come from outside its boundaries (that is, until the 20th century and the introduction of

BELOW *Ceremonial axe-head in bronze dating from the Shang dynasty; bronze casting in Shang China was highly developed, in terms of both technique and decoration.*

19th-century Tibetan cloth painting depicting the gruesome fate awaiting sinners after death.

Marxism-Leninism) was not brought by invaders; Buddhism was introduced to China by traders travelling the Silk Road from India and Central Asia during the 1st century BC.

Two religions, or, more accurately, schools of thought, were already well established in China by this time – Confucianism and Taoism. Confucianism is named after its founder Kongfuzi, or Master Kong, who lived between 551–479 BC, during a period known as 'The Warring States'. After a lifetime spent trying in vain to persuade various nobles and rulers of small states to adopt his ideas on ethics and morals, Confucius died without ever seeing his theories put into prac-

tice. His thoughts were collected by his disciples and published posthumously, although it was not until the Han dynasty that Confucianism became the dominant ideology of the Chinese state.

Confucius argued for a highly structured, hierarchical organization of society in which the family was the mainstay of social cohesion. He believed that a state of harmony could be achieved if everyone was aware of their responsibilities and carried out the duties appropriate to their position. Preaching the virtues of filial piety and the veneration of those who had achieved old age ensured that the extended family remained closely knitted. Although he was non-committal about the existence of supernatural beings, sacrifices were a vital part of Confucius' vision. By carrying out such ceremonies, each was confirmed of his place in the wider scheme of things and reminded of his obligations and duties. For the individual, this took the form of ensuring that one's ancestors were happy and well catered for, both in their dotage and in the afterworld; at state level, the emperor made annual sacrifices to Heaven and Earth. Confucius' concern was a pragmatic one – to ensure the smooth running of a stable, well-ordered state. His philosophy cannot really be said to constitute a 'religion' as it lacks many of the features by which we identify religions, such as a priesthood.

The school of thought known as Taoism came into being about the same time as Confucianism. One of the earliest Taoist texts is a collection of observations, the *Tao Te Ching*, written by the Taoist sage Laozi, around the 6th century BC. At its most philosophical, Taoism argues that there is a natural order in the world that determines the behaviour of all things in existence. Early Taoist thinkers hoped that by studying the world of nature they would discover essential laws. This attention to the spirit of things – particularly naturally occurring phenomena like water or wind – led Taoists into a systematic investigation that became the begin-

ABOVE *17th-century Ming bronze of Laozi, the founder of Taoism. He is shown riding on the water buffalo which carried him away from China to the west.*

RIGHT Summer, *one of a set of paintings by Gong Xian (1652–82), depicting the seasonal changes in the landscape.*

ning of science in China. Later on, Taoism operated on a more popular level; the belief that inanimate objects had their own 'spirit' or 'god' gave rise to a system of worship designed to propitiate these powers which was far removed from the early Taoist principles. Taoist priests also practised the art of *fengshui* (wind and water), a method of determining the positioning of buildings so that they did not offend the spirit of the site. Taoism has had great influence on the development of landscape painting in China. Its preoccupations are reflected in the subject matter of the genre – the scholar gazing out from the shelter of a rustic retreat at pine-clad mountains shrouded in mist has been depicted over and over again.

One of the most important contributions that the introduction of Buddhism made to Chinese life was the concept of transmigration of souls. This belief in cyclical life, the view that souls return to the world in a

RIGHT *The Temple of Heaven in Peking, where the emperor conducted the annual sacrifice to Heaven and the prayers for a good harvest.*

form determined by their behaviour during their previous incarnation, offered some comfort to those who perhaps felt that their present existence left something to be desired. The mythology of Hell owes most to Buddhism: on arriving in the Underworld, the soul comes before Yen Wang, who examines the register recording all good and evil actions. Those who have done good deeds – for example, filial sons or believers – are able to proceed directly to join the Buddha himself, to go to Mount Kunlun, the home of the immortals, or to be reborn immediately as a human being. Sinners are required to come before one of nine judges who mete out the punishment appropriate to the offences committed. The taking

of life was regarded as the most heinous of Buddhist sins; and it brought about a new respect for living things: vegetarianism became popular as a result of Buddhist influence.

The adage 'Confucian in office, Taoist in retirement and Buddhist as death draws near' sums up the pragmatic Chinese approach to religion. If we aim to rationalize and explain, to codify and authenticate these tales, then we will be exasperated and confounded by the tangled knot that is Chinese mythology. If, on the other hand, we can accept them as meaningful and vivid accounts of a way of experiencing the world, of drawing inspiration and comfort, then we enter a realm that will entrance and delight us.

RIGHT *The composition of the character* shou, *longevity, is designed to resemble the Taoist diagram of 'inner circulation'; Qing dynasty rubbing.*

RIGHT *The massive Leshan Buddha near Chngdu, Sichuan province, is carved out of a cliff overlooking a river.*

THE GIANT PANGU

At the beginning of time there was only dark Chaos in the universe. Into this darkness – which took the form of an egg – Pangu, the first living creature, was born. Pangu slept, nurtured safely inside the egg. After many years, when he had grown into a giant, Pangu awoke and stretched, thereby shattering the egg. The lighter, purer parts of the egg rose up to become the sky; the heavier, impure parts sank down to become the earth. This was the beginning of the forces of *yin* and *yang*.

The female element, *yin*, is associated with cold and darkness, the moon and the earth; the male element, *yang*, with light and warmth, the sun and the heavens. (These ancient Chinese concepts of *yin* and *yang* have become familiar to westerners through the popularization of the *I Ching*, or Book of Changes.)

Pangu feared that heaven and earth might merge together again so he placed himself between them, his head supporting the sky and his feet pressing down on the earth. For the next 18,000 years Pangu grew at a rate of 10 feet a day, increasing the distance between the two by the same amount. Eventually both heaven and earth seemed securely fixed at a gap of 30,000 miles, and Pangu fell into an exhausted sleep from which he never awoke. On his death, the different parts of his body were transformed into the natural elements: his breath became the wind and clouds; his voice turned into thunder and lightning; his left eye became the sun and his right the moon; his four limbs and trunk turned into the cardinal directions and the mountains; his blood formed the rivers and his veins the roads and paths; his flesh became trees and soil; the hair on his head became

the stars in heaven, and the skin and hairs on his body turned into grass and flowers; metals and stones were formed from his teeth and bones, and dew from his sweat. And the various parasites on his body became the different peoples of the human race. Thus was the universe created by the giant Pangu.

There are a number of versions of this myth – although broadly similar they differ in detail about the eventual outcome of the parts of Pangu's body.

LEFT *Taoist sages examining a painting of the yin/yang symbol; detail of porcelain dish, Kangxi period, Qing dynasty.*

BELOW *Here the* yin/yang *symbol is surrounded by eight trigrams used in divination. Fuxi, brother of Nugua, is usually credited with their discovery.*

Pangu is also sometimes credited with the power to control the weather, the outlook changing according to his temper. Another account of the origin of the human race is given in the following story:

NUGUA PEOPLES THE WORLD

There was once a goddess who was half human and half snake (some say half dragon). She had the ability to change shape and could do so many times a day. One day, as she wandered through this newly-created world, she felt that although there were many wondrous and beautiful things, it was a lonely place. Nugua yearned for the company of beings like herself, with whom she could talk and laugh. She came to a river and sat down on the bank, gazing at her reflection in the

BELOW *Interior of the Hall of Prayer in the Temple of Heaven, Peking.*

130

water. As she mused, she trailed her hand in the water and scooped up some mud from the riverbed. She kneaded the clay into a little figure, only instead of giving it the tail of a snake, like herself, she fashioned legs so it could stand upright. When this little creature was placed on the ground, it at once came to life, prancing around her and laughing with joy. Nugua was very pleased with her handiwork and determined to populate the whole world with these delightful little people. She worked all that day until nightfall, and started again at dawn the next day. But Nugua soon realized that the task she had set herself was immense, and that she would be exhausted before she had made enough people to fill the world. However, by using her supernatural powers, Nugua found she could achieve her wish. She took a length of vine, dipped it in the mud and then whirled it round in

the air. The drops of mud that flew off the vine were transformed into little people when they touched the ground. Some say that those who had been formed by Nugua herself became the rich and fortunate people of the earth, and those formed from the drops of mud became the ordinary humble folk. Nugua realized that in order to save the human race from becoming extinct when her original people died, they would need a means of reproducing. So she divided the humans into male and female so they could produce future generations without her assistance.

Another story recounts that long ago there were only two people in the world, Nugua and her brother Fuxi. They wanted to marry and produce children, but were afraid to consummate an incestuous marriage without authority from heaven. One day they climbed the sacred Mount Kunlun in the west, and each built a bonfire. The smoke from the two fires mingled together and they took this as a sign that they should indeed become husband and wife. Out of modesty, Nugua made herself a fan of straw and with this she covered her face when they were joined together; it is still the custom today for a bride to hold a fan.

These tales contain a number of features that are common to the creation myths of many cultures. The idea of an egg as the beginning of the world occurs in Indian mythology, and the concept of a single progenitor of the human race can be found in cultures as diverse as those of Greece and Polynesia. Even within China, themes

and motifs occur in numerous guises. A folktale recorded in Hebei province gives Pangu as the maker of the mud figures that became the first humans. And in another story, the union of Tianlong and Diya, attendants of Wenchang, the God of Literature, gives rise to the first humans. The universality of these motifs seems to indicate the similarity of concerns of people the world over, and the degree to which there is a shared human experience.

The structure of the classical Chinese world is indicated in several sources, and from these it is possible to see that there were a number of cosmographies (theories of the universe). Of the *suan ye* school, very little is known, save that its followers believed the sun and stars moved freely about the heavens. One school held that the universe was in the form of an egg, in which the sky was painted inside the upper part of the shell and the earth floated on the ocean that lay in the lower part of the eggshell. A still older tradition, the *zhou bei* school, held that the sky was an inverted bowl rotating around the axis of the Pole Star; the earth was a square underneath the sky, bordered on each side by one of the four seas. The sky was conceived as a solid dome, supported by four or eight pillars or mountains. The fact that the Pole Star does not occupy a central position in the firmament is ingeniously accounted for in the following myth.

BELOW *Vase decorated with the animals that represent the 12 months of the year (5th–6th century AD).*

GONGGONG'S DEFEAT

One day the gods Gonggong and Zhurong decided to do battle in order to find out which was the most powerful. After many days of fierce fighting, in the course of which they tumbled right out of the heavens, Gonggong was defeated. He was so ashamed that he resolved to kill himself by running against Mount Buzhou, one of the mountains holding up the sky. The mountain came off much the worse from this encounter, as a great part of it came crashing down. A jagged hole was torn in the sky, and great crevasses appeared in the earth. From these massive chasms fire and water spewed forth, causing a great flood that covered the surface of the earth. Those who escaped drowning saw their crops and homes consumed by the flames. Nugua, who had given these people life, could not bear to see them suffer so, and quickly acted to restore order. She chose some coloured pebbles from the river bed and melted them down into a viscous substance

RIGHT *Xiwangmu, Queen Mother of the West, rides on a deer holding a peach and a fungus, both symbols of long life (17th-century soapstone carving).*

133

*ABOVE Qing court
robes were embroidered
with dragons, symbols
of imperial authority.*

with which she was able to repair the damage caused to the firmament. In order to be sure that the sky did not collapse again, Nugua slaughtered a giant tortoise and cut off its legs. These she placed at the four points of the compass as extra supports for the heavens. Nugua thus restored order to the world and enabled human beings to carry on their affairs in peace. However, Gonggong's collision with the mountain had caused the heavens to tilt in the direction of the north-west, leaving a void in the south-east. This is the reason all the great rivers of China flow toward the east, emptying their waters in that huge ocean.

It is clear that one of the great concerns of Chinese mythology is the maintenance of order and stability. The belief that natural calamities on earth were caused by disharmony in heaven is reiterated many times in the tales of ancient China, although there is only space here for a few of them.

134

CHANG E'S BETRAYAL

A giant mulberry tree called Fusang grew in the sea beyond the eastern ocean, and in this tree dwelt ten suns. These suns, who were the children of Dijun, God of the East, and Xihe, Goddess of the Sun, took it in turns to go out into the sky. Each morning one of the suns would be ferried across the sky in a chariot driven by his mother, thus bringing warmth and light to the world. One day the ten suns rebelled against the routine and all went into the heavens at once, frolicking across the skies. They enjoyed themselves greatly while they brought disaster down below. The earth dried up, causing all the crops to wither, and even the rocks began to melt. Food became scarce and there was hardly anything to drink. In addition, monsters and wild beasts emerged from the forests in search of prey. Dijun and Xihe took pity on suffering humanity and pleaded with their sons to behave, but without success. In exasperation, Dijun summoned the great archer, Yi, and handed him a quiver of white arrows and a red bow.

LEFT *Bronze mirror decorated with Taoist deities; (3rd century* AD)*.

135

'I depend on you to restore order on earth,' he said. 'Bring my sons under control and slay the wild beasts that are threatening the people.' Yi accepted the challenge and set off, accompanied by his wife, Chang E. It was clear to Yi that he would get nowhere with threats or persuasion so he fitted an arrow to his bow and shot it into the sky. A ball of fire exploded, and the air was filled with golden flames. A moment later, there was a thud as something fell to the ground. People rushed forward and discovered that one of their tormentors had been transformed into a three-legged raven. Yi loosed one arrow after another, each reaching straight to the heart of

BELOW Earthenware figure of a guardian from a Tang dynasty tomb; (early 8th century AD).

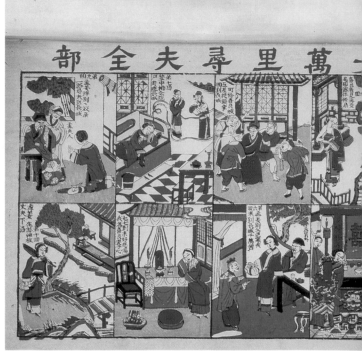

its target. And each time the soul of the sun fell to the ground in the form of a three-legged raven. The air promptly became cooler and, but for the quick thinking of the sage king Yao, all might have been extinguished. Realizing that one sun must remain to provide the earth with light and warmth, Yao counted the number of arrows in Yi's quiver and made sure that Yi would run out before he could shoot down the last sun.

With this task accomplished, Yi now turned his attention to the monsters that still threatened the earth. With great skill and bravery, Yi despatched one fearsome beast after another until at last there was peace.

Yi was looked upon as a great hero and everyone was extremely grateful to him for saving them from a terrible fate. With the sounds of praise still ringing in his ears, Yi returned to heaven with his wife Chang E to report on his successful mission. But instead of welcoming him with open arms, Yi found that the god Dijun had shunned him.

'Although I cannot deny that you have only done my bidding, I find that I cannot bear to look upon you, you who have killed my sons. You and

ABOVE Early 20th-century New Year woodblock print telling the story of Meng Qiang nu, whose husband was enlisted to build the Great Wall during the Qin dynasty (221–206 BC). When he failed to return she set off to find him. On hearing that he was among the many who had perished in the course of the construction of the Wall, she began to weep and her tears caused the Wall to collapse. The beginning of the sorry tale is told here, starting on the right-hand side, moving top to bottom.

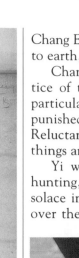

Chang E must leave heaven and return to earth, to those you served so well.'

Chang E was furious at the injustice of this decision, and felt it was particularly unfair that she should be punished for her husband's actions. Reluctantly they packed up their things and moved down to earth.

Yi was able to fill his days with hunting, but Chang E could find no solace in their new home and mulled over their sorry state endlessly. 'Now we have been sent to live in the world of men, and one day, like them, we will die and have to descend to the Underworld. Our only hope is to go to the Queen Mother of the West, who lives on Mount Kunlun, and obtain the elixir of immortality from her.' Yi set off at once and, after many travails, he at last entered the presence of the Queen Mother. The Queen Mother was moved by Yi's sad story and agreed to help him and Chang E.

LEFT *Cakes in the shape of the full harvest moon are eaten during the mid-autumn festival.*

'This box contains enough elixir to give eternal life to two people, although you will still have to remain in the world of men. To obtain complete immortality you would need to take twice as much. Guard the box well, for all I have is contained therein.'

Yi returned home with the precious box and entrusted it to the care of his wife, planning to wait until a suitably auspicious day to take the drug. But Chang E mused, 'Why should I not take the whole amount, and be restored to my former status of goddess.

After all, I have been punished quite without justification.' Immediately after she had taken the elixir, Chang E could feel her feet rise from the ground. Up and up she began to float, out of the window and through the night air.

'On second thoughts,' she said to herself, 'perhaps it would not be such a good idea to return straight to heaven: the gods might criticise me for not sharing the elixir with my husband.'

Chang E resolved to go first to the moon, which was shining overhead in

the clear, starlit sky. When she arrived on the moon Chang E found it to be a desolate place, empty except for a hare under a cassia tree. But when she tried to move on, Chang E found that her powers had deserted her and she was doomed to keep her lonely vigil to the end of time.

Yi was shocked and saddened when he found that his wife had betrayed him. He took on a pupil, Peng Meng, perhaps hoping that his skills at least would not die with him. Peng Meng studied hard and eventually reached the point where only Yi was better than him at archery. Peng Meng grew increasingly jealous of his master's superiority, and one day, in an opportune moment, killed him.

A very popular and well-known myth concerning stars in the sky is that of the ox herd and the weaving girl, who respectively represent the stars Altair and Vega, on either side of the Milky Way. This story holds particular significance for parted lovers; indeed, a husband and wife who have been assigned to work in different parts of the country are referred to in such terms.

ABOVE *Embroidered pillow end showing Chang E on her flight to the moon.*

Indian Mythology

All over India millions of tiny oil lamps are lit as dusk falls. They shine out, row upon row of them, from rooftops and windowsills. It is autumn, the night of the great festival of Diwali. Children settle down around their mothers or grandmothers to hear the story of Lakshmi, the fickle goddess of wealth and good fortune. Hearing this tale, and countless others, at their mother's knee is their entertainment. They are absorbed in a rich fantasy world of gods and demons, princes and princesses, friendly animals and exciting adventures. Their psyches have free range over ideas of good and evil, exploring ways of living life and of facing death. They find these stories in books, films, theatre, dance, sculpture and painting, and in comics, but nothing compares with the power of an ancient tale directly told, handed down by word of mouth from generation to generation for thousands of years.

Vishnu, the most popular of the Hindu deities, and his consort, Lakshmi, ride on the bird-god Garuda; (18th-century Bundi painting from Rajasthan).

There is always a moral to the story: how to be the perfect wife or husband, how to be reborn as a better person, how to behave toward others, how to keep the gods happy with sacrifice and celebration. Much of Indian mythology holds a religious context, which speaks in particular to those holy men and women, priests, hermits and wandering ascetics who are searching for the key to the ultimate nature of reality, and for the way to escape the endless cycle of rebirth.

For the historian, the language and images of the ancient mythological texts present the ancient history of the land. The migrations of the Aryan peoples into India can be followed by tracing the burial and cremation practices of the region, as described in the ancient Vedic hymns. The cultural influences of the indigenous Dravidian peoples can be seen in the increased importance of the goddesses in subsequent sacred texts. The struggles of rival dynasties are vividly described in the great battles of the epic poems, the *Ramayana* and the *Mahabharata*. Indeed, Indian mythology is like a mirror that shows their hearts' desire to all who look into it.

Most of the stories in this introduction are Hindu tales, but other religions have not been overlooked. The story of the life of the Buddha, for example, is included. Although he is an historical figure, his life itself has been turned into an elaborate myth involving gods and demons, even though the Buddhist doctrine is atheistic. The Buddha is even sometimes described as an incarnation of Vishnu.

In the Indian Hindu tradition, the lives of famous holy men, saints, and the founders of other great religions are elaborated in similar ways. For instance, Mahavira, the founder of Jainism, was born after his mother had a visionary dream. The astrologers forecast his coming and the gods closely observed his young life full of heroic feats.

Traditional biographers also elaborated the life of the founder of Sik-hism, Guru Nanak, who lived from 1469 to 1539. Although he believed in only one God, his birth was said to be witnessed by millions of gods who foretold his future as a great man. This greatness is exhibited in various feats of magic. For example, when his disciple Mardana was hungry, Guru Nanak turned poison berries into edible fruits. The story of his enlightenment is that he disappeared while bathing in the river and was presumed dead: After three days he returned and explained that he had been with God. His first words on his return were said to be 'There is neither Hindu or Muslim, so whose path shall I fol-

BELOW *The Jain saint Parsvanartha; (11th-century sculpture from Orissa). The austerity of Jain doctrine is expressed in the simple, continuous form.*

low? I will follow God's path. God is neither Hindu nor Muslim, and the path I follow is God's'. But even in the *Adi Granth*, or Original Collection of the hymns of the Gurus, the one God is sometimes described with reference to the Hindu deities: 'He, the One, is Himself Brahma, Vishnu and Shiva'.

Similarly, the animal stories of the Buddhist Jataka tales use all kinds of folk tales that have been used to illustrate Buddhist values. Some of these tales have been floating around the world for centuries and turn up in different forms in Homer, Boccaccio and Chaucer. They can be claimed by anyone! (Some students of Indian

LEFT A *Jain saint in the arms of his mother; (11th-century stone icon from western India).*

143

mythology believe that Hinduism claimed the epic poems of the *Rama-yana* and the *Mahabharata* in the same way by inserting sacred texts, such as the *Bhaghavad Gita,* at appropriate points in the story.)

'Each myth celebrates the belief that the universe is boundlessly vari-ous, that everything occurs simulta-neously, that all possibilities may exist without excluding each other' (Wendy O'Flaherty, *The Origins of Evil in Indian Mythology*). This is also a good way to describe the Indian subcontinent itself. It is geographically diverse, with the great Himalayan mountains in the north, rice- and wheat-growing plains, desert and tropical jungle, high, tea-growing plateaux and low-lying coastal areas with palm trees where the land is criss-crossed with waterways. The climate is extreme, the hot season brought to an abrupt end by the heavy monsoon rains. Although 8 out of 10 Indians are Hindus, India is the home of many followers of other great world religions, including Islam and Christianity.

IN THE
BEGINNING

Some of the creation myths are very abstract, struggling with the con-cepts of existence and non-existence as in this extract from the hymn of creation from the *Rig Veda.*

'Neither not-being nor being was there at that time; there was no air-filled space nor was there the sky which is beyond it. What enveloped all? And where? Under whose protection? What was the unfathomable deep water? . . . Upon it rose up, in the beginning, desire, which was the mind's first seed. Having sought in their hearts, the wise ones discovered, through deliberation, the bond of be-ing and nonbeing . . . Whereupon this creation has issued, whether he has made it or whether he has not –

ABOVE *Three-headed icon of Brahma, the creator; early 11th-century Chola sculpture from south India.*

he who is the superintendent of this world in the highest heaven – he alone knows, or, perhaps, even he does not know.'

There are other stories where the gods actively create the world. The story of Prajapati, who rose from the primordial waters weeping as he was lonely and did not know why he had been born, for example. The tears that fell into the water became the earth, the tears that he wiped away became the sky and the air. Then he created people and spirits, night and day, the seasons and finally death.

In a creation myth using the con-cept of the egg – also found in Chinese and many many other mythologies – Brahma is the creator. The golden egg grew from a seed floating on the cosmic ocean for a year, and shone with the lustre of the sun. Brahma emerged from the egg and split himself into two people, one male and one female, the incestuous union of these two being the creative force. Brahma is also called Narayana (he who came from the waters) who is described as lying on a banyan leaf, floating on primeval waters sucking his toe – a symbol of eternity.

One fascinating creation myth

RIGHT *The Cosmic Egg according to Hindu theory; 18th-century painting (gouache on paper) from Rajasthan. At the bottom is Vishnu, reclining on the cosmic serpent. From his navel protrudes the lotus upon which sits Brahma. At the top is Vaikuntha, or paradise, where Krishna dwells.*

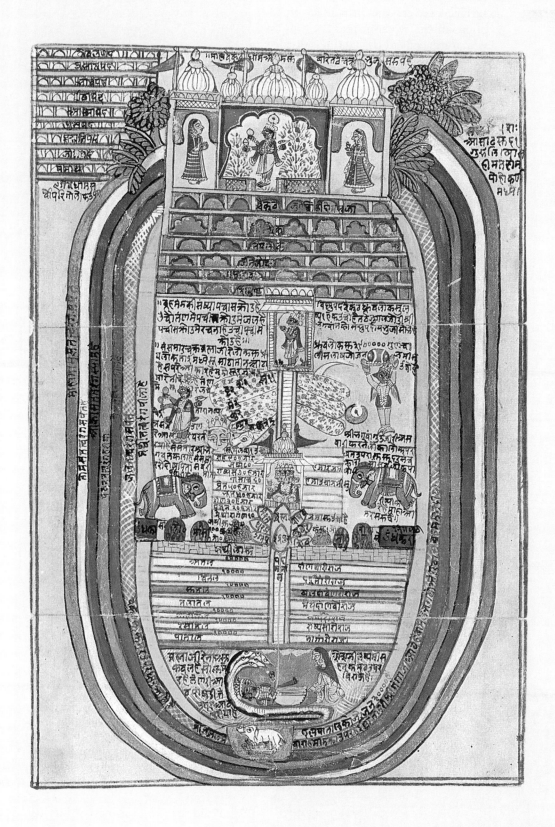

involves the sacrifice of Purusha, the cosmic person. The description of the sacrifice evokes the ritualistic atmosphere of the worship and the way in which the body of the victim is divided up is said to be the origin of the caste system. This is a translation of some of the verses of the Hymn to the Cosmic Person. It is part of the *Rig Veda*, the earliest book of the songs of the ancient seers which was composed by the Vedic Aryans who came into India from central Asia. They overran the already established Indus Valley civilization. The Vedic period spans approximately 2500 to 600 BC.

Indra was the most prominent god in the *Rig Veda*. He is identified with

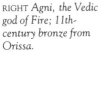

RIGHT *Agni, the Vedic god of Fire; 11th-century bronze from Orissa.*

thunder and wields the *vajra* or thunderbolt, and his most significant deed is the slaying of the demon Vritra who holds captive the sun and the rain. This deed can be seen to represent either the conquest of India by Aryan warriors led by their champion, Indra; or as the cosmological allegory of the conquest of chaos and the release of the life forces of water, heat and light.

Agni is second only to Indra in the Vedic pantheon. He is the personification and deification of fire. His three forms are terrestial as fire, atmospheric as lightning, and celestial as the sun. He is a messenger between mortals and the gods and therefore particularly important as the sacrificial fire.

A thousand headed is the cosmic
  person.
With a thousand eyes and feet,
Enveloping the earth on all sides,
And going ten fingers beyond.

When they divided the cosmic person,
Into how many parts did they divide
  him?
What did they call his mouth? What
  his arms?
What did they call his legs? What his
  feet?
His mouth was the priestly class,

ABOVE *Impression of a Steatite seal from Mohenjo-Daro showing a humped Brahmani bull (Indus valley civilization c.2500–2000 BC). Seals like this one are the earliest art objects in India. Less than 2ins (4cms) high, the fine craftsmanship betrays a keen observation of animal form. Frequent portrayal of bulls on such seals suggest that they were religious symbols.*

RIGHT *Putusa, the thousand-headed cosmic person, standing on Vishnu; 17th-century Nepali painting (gouache on cloth).*

The sky came from his head.
From his feet came earth, from his
ears the four regions.
Thus they formed the worlds.

(John M. Koller, *The Indian Way*)

MEASURING THE COSMOS

The legend which provides the key to Hindu cosmology and introduces us to the cyclical theory of time and to the theory of the transmigration of souls is the myth of the four Ages of Man.

The four Ages, or Yugas, are named after four throws of the dice. The Krita Yuga was the perfect age when there were no gods or demons, people were saintly and there was no disease. The Treta Yuga was when sacrifices began and virtue lessened a quarter. The Dwapara Yuga was a decadent age when virtue lessened one half and there came desire, disease and calamities. And the Kali Yuga is the degenerate age when only one quarter of virtue remains and people are wicked. The latter is, of course, the age that we live in.

The ancient mathematicians worked out that these four ages spread over 4,320,000 years, and that 1,000 of these periods equals one day of Brahma. At the end of each 'day' (*kalpa*), Brahma sleeps for a night of equal length, and before he falls asleep the universe is destroyed by fire and flood and becomes as it was in the beginning. He creates anew when he wakes the next morning. A year of Brahma is 360 *kalpas* and he endures for 100 years – and that is half of his existence. After another 100 years of chaos and disorder, a new Brahma will arise to create a new universe, and so the cycle will begin again.

This eternal cycle of creation and destruction is the backdrop to the eternal cycle of birth and death that those who believe in reincarnation

His arms the warrior-princes.
His legs were the producers,
His feet the servant class.

From his mind was born the moon,
From his eye was born the sun.
Indra and Agni came from his mouth,
And the wind was born of his breath

From his navel came the atmosphere,

THE SPREAD OF BUDDHISM

The painting below is from a 19th-century Burmese book of illustrations of Buddhist heavens and hells. Buddhism has evolved according to national cultures to a bewildering extent: the Zen Buddhism of Japan, the Lamaistic Buddhism of Tibet, and Burmese and Sri Lankan Buddhism all have different emphases, Buddhist sects having quickly sprung up after the fifth century BC, basing their philosophies upon specific scriptures. Thus Zen Buddhism is based upon meditation in order to achieve 'sudden enlightenment', while Tibetan Buddhism, which arrived in the country and flourished in the 7th century AD, emphasizes the practices of the Tantra. Buddhism is divided into two main schools: the Theravada, or Hinayana, which predominates in Sri Lanka, Burma and Southeast Asia, and the Mahayana, found in China, Korea and Japan. A chief distinction is the Mahayana veneration of the Bodhisattva, a person who refuses to enter nirvana and escape the cycle of death and rebirth – even though he has earned the right – until all others have been similarly enlightened and saved.

LEFT *Painting of a scene from the epic poem the Ramayana.*

nature. Belief in a creator is considered an evil doctrine and makes no sense because '. . . If he were transcendant he would not create, for he would be free; nor if involved in transmigration, for then he would not be almighty.' (*Sources of Indian Tradition* ed. T. de Bary)

Although the great ascetic philosophy of Jainism rejected much of Hindu thought, the two beliefs shared one vision of the cosmos. The emphasis Jains laid on wisdom and teaching preserved and created many important learned texts on mathematics and other objects and also formed a body of popular literature in many different Indian languages. They have produced many beautiful maps of the cosmos, full of measurements and fine details.

Brahma, Shiva and Vishnu are the three most important of the Hindu gods. Brahma, the creator, is not worshipped as a personal god today and there is only one temple dedicated to him in the whole of India. His wife is Sarasvati, the goddess of learning and the patroness of arts, sciences and speech. Her earthly embodiment is the river Sarasvati, and as the river she presides over religious festivals

BELOW *Ephemeral clay figures of Sarasvati, the goddess of learning, wisdom, eloquence, music and the arts. She carries a Vina (a stringed instrument) and is mounted on a swan. During worship the clay figurines are carried in procession through the streets and then immersed in the Ganges or a nearby river or tank. Sarasvati is a popular deity in Bengal.*

must endure. The atheistic Jains reject the doctrines of a divine creator. For them natural laws provide a more satisfactory explanation. They believe that the world is not created but is without beginning or end, existing under the compulsion of its own

LEFT *Stone icon of Harihari, or Shiva and Vishnu combined, (c. 1000 AD).*

and gives fertility and wisdom to the earth. She may be portrayed holding the stringed instrument, the *vina*, a lotus bud, a book, a rosary, a drum or a stick of sugar cane.

Shiva is a very ancient god. He is still extremely popular today and is often worshipped in the form of a *lingam*, a stone phallus. He represents the underlying unity of existence in which all opposites are reconciled. He is creator and destroyer. As Lord of the Dance he dances out the awesome rhythms of creation and destruction, but as well as being a bringer of death, he conquers death and disease and is invoked to cure sickness. He is the great ascetic who has conquered desire, smeared with ashes and haunting the cremation grounds. But at the

RIGHT *Shiva the cosmic dancer; he dances the endless rhythms of creation and destruction. The significance of Shiva's dance becomes clearer if one remembers that a dance is at once a free expression of the will and an action directed by exterior laws – if you like, by the rhythm of the music of time. Thus Shiva is a god, but he is defined by larger ineffable patterns.*

same time he is erotic, the great lover and passionate husband.

To the philosopher these opposing qualities are a paradox, but to the worshipper they represent the richness of existence and the totality of the divine being. The ultimate reconciliation of the conflicts embodied by Shiva is brought about when half his body becomes female and half of him remains male. There are many stories about Shiva and his exploits. In this one he safeguards immortality:

LEFT *The Divine Couple, Shiva and Parvati, with their children at the burning-ground; behind them is Shiva's mount, the bull Nandi. Shiva's son, the elephant-headed Ganesh, helps him to make a necklace of skulls. Parvati holds the six-headed son Karttikeya; (18th-century).*

BELOW LEFT *Hindu temple sculpture of Shiva and Parvati as one, half male, half female figure.*

BELOW *Shiva Nataraja,
Lord of the Dance
(10th-century Chola
bronze from Madras
state, southern India);
one of the most famous
of all Hindu icons, still
reproduced to this day.
The legend associated
with this image involves
the subjugation of ten
thousand heretical
holymen. They sent a
tiger against him but
Shiva flayed it and took
its skin as a cape.
A poisonous snake
attacked him and he
just hung it round his
neck as a garland.
Next a black dwarf
attacked him with a
club, but Shiva put
one foot on him and
danced until the dwarf
and the holymen
acknowledged him as
the supreme master.
The drum he holds in
his upper right hand
beats out the rhythm of
creation. The single
flame in his upper left
hand is the flame of*

SHIVA'S BLUE THROAT

Following the advice of Vishnu, the gods and the demons were churning the celestial ocean of milk to obtain from it the nectar of immortality. For a churning rope they used the divine serpent Vasuki, and the great mountain Mandara was the churning rod. They churned furiously for 100 years. Among the first gifts of the celestial ocean were the beautiful goddess Lakshmi, who rose from a lotus flower floating on the rippling waves, and the divine cow Surabhi whose son Nandi, the snow-white bull, later became Shiva's companion and mount. The next gift was a crescent moon which Shiva snatched from the waves and placed on his forehead. Suddenly a terrible poisonous venom began gushing from the serpent's 1,000 mouths, threatening all existence. Moved by the request of the great Vishnu, Shiva swallowed the poison

as if it were the nectar of immortality, thereby saving existence from extermination. The serpent's poison was harmless to the great Shiva but the venom stained his throat dark blue.

In painting Shiva is frequently portrayed with a blue throat and has acquired the epithet Nilakantha, or Blue Throat. A popular image of Shiva is that of Lord of the Dance, and he is frequently surrounded by a ring of sacred fire. This icon represents his five divine functions: creation, preservation, destruction, revelation (of the concealment of ignorance), and release (from rebirth).

But Shiva is most often worshipped as the *lingam*. The *lingam* is usually a cylinder of dark, shiny stone with a curved top set in a circular receptacle, or *yoni*, the symbol of female sexuality. Sometimes there are carvings of the five heads of Shiva on the *lingam*. It represents not only sexuality and the male creative force, but also chastity, as the seed is contained and controlled by yogic meditations. Mythology thrives on such paradoxes and there are many stories of the conflicts and

*destruction. His lower
right hand is held in a
gesture of benediction
to his devotees. This is
reaffirmed by his lower
left hand which is
drooping in imitation of
an elephant's trunk and
pointing towards his
upraised left foot, a
symbolic gesture
promising release from
Samsara, or rebirth, to
his followers. His right
foot crushes the demon
of ignorance
symbolized by the
dwarf. The ring of
sacred fire represents
both the cosmos itself
and also the final
release from Samsara,
by its association with
the cremation ground.*

ABOVE *Stone Shiva icon
in the form of a
Lingam symbolizing
divine power. The face
carved on it represents
the indwelling deity.
A lingam occupies a
sacred spot in all
temples dedicated to
Shiva (7th–8th
century, Kashmir).*

struggles of Shiva as the erotic ascetic and of the problems of his unconventional married life. This tale tells of the rivalry between Shiva and Daksha, the father of his wife Sati. It is with reference to this story that the name Sati is given to the horrendous practice of throwing a widow on her husband's funeral pyre, imbuing what is an act of social and economic expediency with a ritual significance.

THE DEATH OF SATI

Daksha was holding a grand sacrifice to which all the gods were invited except Shiva. Sati was furious and decided to go since it was her own father's house. Shiva was pleased at

Ithyphallic figure of Shiva in his creative aspect; it is the double nature of Hindu gods that sometimes puzzles western observers (it is this confounding of opposites, this apparent lack of moral or metaphysical polarities, that destroys Mrs Moore in E. M. Forster's novel A Passage to India.

ABOVE *Shiva walking with the bull Nandi, followed by his consort Parvati; (c. 1730–40 painting from Mandi, north-west India).*

RIGHT *Stone icon of Shiva and Parvati.*

her loyalty and fervour but he warned her to be strong. 'Daksha will insult me and if you are unable to tolerate his insults, I fear you may come to harm,' he said. Sati arrived at the sacrifice and told her father, 'My lord is deep in meditation, I come alone.' Daksha laughed, seeing his chance to heap insults on his great rival. 'It is a disgrace for a god to wear filthy rags, to adorn himself with snakes and dance like a madman. I could never understand how a daughter of mine could wish for a creature like that for a husband.'

Sati, trembling with rage, denounced her father before the assembled gods. Since Shiva had instructed her not to take revenge she immolated herself on the sacrificial

The extremely popular elephant-headed god Ganesh, also known as 'The Remover of Obstacles'. His nature is gentle and affectionate and his image is found installed over the main entrance of many Indian homes to ward off evil. Symbolically, his round fat body contains the whole universe, his bended trunk can remove obstacles and his four arms represent the categories that the world can be divided into (that is the four castes). The sculpture is from Uttar Pradesh, c. 750 AD.

fire. Shiva's rage and torment at the loss of his beloved wife created a fearful demon who destroyed everyone who had been at the ceremony. Only when Vishnu interceded did Shiva relent and bring them all back to life. Daksha finally acknowledged that Shiva was a greater god than he, and as a sign of his foolishness he wore the head of a goat. Shiva fell into a profound meditation, waiting for the time when his beloved would be re-incarnated as Parvati and be his wife again.

One of the children of Shiva and Parvati is Ganesh, the elephant-headed god. He is the general of Shiva's army, the patron of learning, the giver of good fortune and a popular deity today. At the beginning of books he is invoked by poets, his image is placed on the ground when a new house is built and he is honoured before a journey is begun or any business undertaken. This is the story of how he came to have an elephant's head:

THE ELEPHANT-HEADED GOD

Shiva had been away for years and Parvati was bored and lonely. She decided to make herself a baby to play with and fashioned a small roly-poly boy out of clay. One day when Parvati was bathing in a pool she asked her

RIGHT *The goddess
Durga killing the
buffalo demon
Mahisha. In her eight
arms she carries
weapons lent to her by
the gods; (13th-century
stone sculpture from
Orissa).*

son Ganesh to make sure no one disturbed her. Shiva arrived home at that moment and started to look for Parvati. The boy, not realizing who it was, stopped him from going near the pool. Furious at being opposed, Shiva immediately cut off the boy's head with his sword. Parvati's grief knew no bounds, she screamed and threw herself sobbing on the ground. To placate her, Shiva sent 1,000 goblins, demons and imps to look for the head of a male child. They searched all night but finding each baby animal asleep facing his mother they did not have the heart to cut off his head. Finally they found a baby elephant who was sleeping with his head turned away from his mother so his trunk didn't get entangled with his mother's and prevent them snuggling close together. Immediately Shiva's goblins removed his head and brought it to him. As he fitted the elephant's head onto his child's body he breathed life into it and waited for Parvati's reaction. To his surprise, she was delighted.

Shiva's bride is a perfect wife in the forms of Sati and Parvati, but like Shiva, she also has her horrible forms. As Durga she is the beautiful and ferocious warrior goddess, and as the hideous personification of death and destruction she is Kali, the black earth mother. As Kali, she is usually depicted naked save for a girdle of giant's heads suspended from her waist. She has long, flowing hair and a long necklace of giant's skulls around her neck. Like Shiva, she has a flaming third eye on her forehead. She is usually depicted with four arms: in one she holds a weapon, and in another the dripping head of a giant; two empty hands are raised to bless her worshippers. She is covered by a tiger skin and her long tongue protrudes, thirsty for blood. To her devotees, Kali is a divine and loving mother who reveals to them the reality of mortality. She not only destroys demons but also death itself. She appeals especially to those who find the mother–child relationship and

symbol more satisfying as a revelation of the divine reality:

KALI'S DANCE OF DEATH

A wicked monster was ravaging the world. He seemed invincible because every drop of blood that he spilled came to life and became 1,000 more demons ready to battle. The gods summoned Kali and asked her to destroy the monster. Leaping into battle, the terrible goddess slayed 1,000 demons with her whirling sword. As she killed them she drank their blood,

RIGHT Kali, the mother goddess in her horrible form; (9th-century stone icon from Orissa). She is holding a sword and wearing a garland of skulls.

159

licking up the drops before they could touch the ground and produce more demons. Finally only the original monster was left and she consumed him in one gulp. Beginning her victory dance she became more and more frenzied and out of control, threatening all creation. Fearing that the universe would be destroyed, the gods came to her husband Shiva and begged him to intercede and stop her wild dance of destruction. But she paid no heed even to him, until in desperation he threw himself down before her. She began to dance on his body. Eventually, realizing what she was doing, she came out of her trance and stopped dancing. Thus the universe was saved from the ravages of the mad dance of Kali.

Vishnu is the most widely worshipped of the Hindu gods. He is all-

ABOVE *Vishnu in his
10th and future
incarnation as the
white horse Kalkin;
(c. 1780 miniature
from Bilaspur, Madhya
Pradesh).*

LEFT *Vishnu
worshipped in five
manifestations; an
illustration from the
Hindu text* Vishnu
Samabranahama.
*(17th- century
painting).*

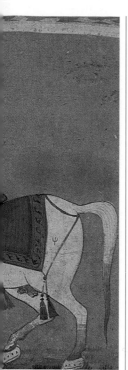

pervading, the preserver of the world, and his function is to ensure the triumph of good against evil. To this end he comes to earth on many occasions in different incarnations. The most famous are his lives as the epic heroes Krishna and Rama, but there are also the fish, the tortoise, the boar, the man-lion, the dwarf, Parashurama, Buddha and Kalkin.

These incarnations show how Hinduism has taken over and absorbed popular folk deities and the tales associated with them. Vishnu is often depicted with four arms. He holds in his hands the characteristic symbols of the wheel (the powers of creation and destruction), the conch shell (associated with the origin of existence through its spiral form, its sound, and its connection with water), and the club (authority or the power of know-

ledge), and his fourth hand has an upraised palm expressing reassurance.

Vishnu's consort in all his incarnations is Lakshmi, the popular goddess of wealth and good fortune. She is also known as the fickle one as she is a wanderer who never stays long with anyone. During the festival of Diwali in the late autumn, thousands of tiny lanterns are lit all over India, houses are cleaned and decorated until they too are sparkling, and fireworks are let off. All this is to please Lakshmi who is wandering from house to house looking for somewhere to spend the night and blessing with prosperity all those houses that are well lit.

In his incarnation as a fish, Matsya, Vishnu saved Manu from a great flood so that his descendants could people the world:

RIGHT *Vishnu in his Lion incarnation.*

FAR RIGHT *Vishnu in his Boar incarnation, lifting the earth-goddess Bhumi from the primeval ocean; (12th-century Chaunan-style stone icon from Punjab).*

VISHNU
THE PRESERVER

While bathing in the river one day, Manu found a tiny fish. The fish begged him to rescue him from the other big fish who wanted to eat him. Manu scooped up the little fish and took him home in an earthenware pot. but Matsya, the fish, soon grew too big for the pot and Manu dug a pond for him to live in. When Matsya had grown too big for the pond he asked Manu to take him to the ocean and release him. As Manu tossed Matsya into the ocean, the fish turned and spoke to him. He warned Manu that in a year's time there would be a great flood, and told him to build a ship to save himself as the whole world would be submerged. Manu did as Matsya had told him and when the flood came he took refuge in his ship, praising Matsya for saving him. As the storms grew fierce and dangerous, Matsya appeared again. Now an enormous fish with golden scales and a horn, he attached the ship's cable to his horn and towed it along. Pulling the ship behind him, Matsya swam for many years until they reached mount Hemavat, the top of which was still above the water. Manu moored the ship to the mountain to await the end of the flood. Before he left, Matsya announced that he was really Vishnu the Preserver and had saved Manu from the flood in order that he might create new plants, animals and people for the world.

Krishna is the most beloved of all the Hindu gods. For his worshippers he embodies divine beauty, joy, and love. The playfulness of the divine child and the charming and tender love of the divine youth draw the devotees into the loving embrace of the supreme God. This is the story of the life of Krishna:

BELOW Vishnu in his fish incarnation, Matsya.

THE YOUNG
KRISHNA

The gods wanted someone to destroy the evil king Kans of Mathura, so Vishnu resolved to be born as the eighth son of the king's sister Devaki. King Kans was warned of this scheme and he imprisoned Devaki and her husband Vasudev and killed each of their sons as they were born. But when Krishna was born Vishnu appeared to the couple and told them to exchange their baby son for the newborn daughter of a cowherd couple, Yasodha and Nanda, who lived in the village of Gokul across the river Yamuna. Vasudev found the doors of the prison miraculously open and set

ABOVE *Radha and Krishna in the Grove; (18th-century Pahari painting from the hill state of Kangra in Punjab). All nature rejoices in the couple's bliss and their embrace is echoed by the vine which encircles the tree in the foreground.*

off for Gokul with the child. He had to cross the river Yamuna in a terrible storm and feared for their safety. The baby Krishna touched the water with his foot and the waves parted, letting them through. Vasudev left the baby with Yasodha, who brought him up as her own son, and returned to jail with the baby girl who was no threat to King Kans. However, the king found out that Krishna had been saved and sent a demon nurse called Patoona to destroy him. The demon managed to deceive Yasodha and Nanda, but when she gave her breast to the baby Krishna he sucked and sucked until he had sucked all of Patoona's life away. As a child Krishna was playful and mischievous. Innocent and obedient in his mother's presence, he missed no opportunity for mischief when her back was turned. He untied the village calves and pulled their tails, mocked and laughed at his elders and teased

RIGHT *The young Krishna striking the cow with his cowherd's flask; his half-brother Balaram stands behind. The scene takes place beneath a Bo-tree; (10th-century stone relief carving).*

BELOW *Krishna subdues the snake demon by dancing on its head; (19th-century fragment of a temple painting from Madras).*

little babies until they cried, urinated in neighbours' houses and stole butter and sweets. But Yasodha and Nanda, who have no control over him, just laughed at his antics. When Krishna was about 12 he slew Kaliya, the five-headed serpent king who had been killing chickens, goats and cattle. He also destroyed the demon Trinavarta who was sent by King Kans disguised as a whirlwind. As a youth, Krishna enchanted and intoxicated the cow-herd women with his flute playing. He teased them and made love to them. His favourite was the beautiful Radha, who took many risks to meet her dark lover:

How can I describe his relentless
    flute,
which pulls virtuous women from
    their homes
and drags them by their hair to
    Krishna
as thirst and hunger pull the doe to
    the snare?

Chaste ladies forget their lords,
wise men forget their wisdom,
and clinging vines shake loose from
    their trees,
hearing that music.

(David R. Kinsley, *The Sword and the Flute*).

BELOW *Gopis (cowherds) begging Krishna to return their clothes. He has stolen them while the Gopis are bathing to tease them; (18th-century Kangra painting).*

Eventually, stories of Krishna's exploits reached King Kans and he resolved to try and kill him again.

THE WRESTLING CONTEST

The king announced a wrestling match and challenged the local young men to try and beat the court champions. His plan was to lure Krishna and his brother Balaram into the city and, pretending that it was an accident, release a wild elephant in their path. He felt sure that they would not survive such an encounter. Krishna and Balaram seized the chance to show off their prowess at wrestling and came to the city on the day of the festivities. When their turn came, they entered the ring to be faced by a wild elephant charging towards them

BELOW *A highly stylized 18th-century portrait of Radha from Kishangarh in Rajasthan. The painter Nihal Chand is thought to have derived this style from the poetry of his patron, Raja Savant Singh, describing his own beloved whose nose was 'curved and sharp like the thrusting saru cypress plant'.*

RIGHT *Rama with his bow; (16th-century bronze from Madras).*

trumpeting in fury. Without hesitating, Krishna leapt upon the elephant, and putting his mighty arms around its neck he squeezed until the creature fell beneath him dead. The crowd cheered and King Kans, more furious and frightened than ever, sent his fearsome champions into the ring. But they were no match for the brothers. Krishna soon broke the neck of the first, and Balaram squeezed the second in a great bear hug until his heart burst. Then Krishna leapt upon King Kans and flung him against the wall, killing him in front of the assembled crowds. He then freed his parents and his grandfather, who was the rightful king.

Many more exploits and marriages of Krishna are recounted in the epic poem, the *Mahabharata*. It is into his mouth that tradition puts the *Bhagavad Gita*, one of the most sacred books of modern Hinduism.

Rama is the hero of the other great epic, the *Ramayana*, and another incarnation of Vishnu, sent to earth to kill the demon Ravana. His wife, Sita, is considered to be the perfect wife and her behaviour is held up to young girls to emulate. Sita was abducted by

BELOW *A 20th-century depiction of Hanuman, the monkey god, causing mischief among people; note the flames he carries (top right). In the story related (right), Hanuman is protected by Agni, the god of fire.*

the demon Ravana and carried off to his Kingdom of Lanka and the distraught Rama went in search of her. In the forest he enlisted the help of the monkey god Hanuman. In this extract Hanuman uses his magic powers to reach Lanka and discovers Sita:

HANUMAN THE MONKEY GOD

Hanuman learned from Sampati, the brother of the king of the vultures, that Sita had been carried off to the distant island of Lanka, a hundred leagues over the southern ocean. Being the son of Vayu, the wind god, Hanuman resolved to use his powers to leap over the sea. He filled his lungs with sea wind and, with a mighty roar, rushed to the top of a mountain. Assuming a gigantic form, he leapt into the air and sped across the sea like an arrow. But his path through the air was impeded by demons. Surasa opened her enormous jaws to catch him, but he quickly shrunk to the size of a man's thumb and leapt in and out of her gaping mouth before she could close it. Next his shadow was grabbed by the she-dragon Sinhika who wanted to devour him. But he wounded and killed her and carried on to the island. Arriving at night he turned himself into a cat and crept stealthily around the sumptuous palace looking for Sita. Creeping up the jewelled stairways of gold and silver he came across the women's chamber. The perfumed forms asleep seemed like a wreath of lotus blooms awaiting the kiss of the morning sun. Outside, in a grove of Asoka trees, Hanuman saw the long-lost Sita. Guarded by fierce and ugly demons with the heads of dogs and pigs, she was without fear. Although Ravana came daily, threatening her with torture and death if she would not marry him, she rejected him. She would die before she was unfaithful to Rama.

LEFT *Hanuman, the monkey god, from a Vaishnavite shrine; (11th-century Tamilwork bronze from Sri Lanka).*

167

LEFT *The conception of
the Buddha, Queen
Maya's dream of the
white elephant.
Gandhara style
sculpture c. 2nd
century* AD.

Hanuman secretly approached the beautiful, sorrowing Sita and showed her Rama's ring that he was carrying. He offered to carry her away, but her modesty prevented her from touching the body of any man except her husband. Instead she gave him a jewel from her hair and begged him to tell Rama that she had only two months to live if he did not rescue her. Before he left, Hanuman decided to destroy as much of Ravana's kingdom as he could. Turning himself back into a giant monkey he started to uproot trees and devastate the countryside, but he was taken prisoner by Ravana's son, the mighty Indrajit, who shot him with a magic serpent arrow. As a gesture of defiance, Ravana set Hanuman's tail on fire and sent him back to Rama as an envoy. But Sita prayed that he would not burn and Agni, the god of fire, spared him. As he escaped from the kingdom of Lanka, Hanuman managed to accomplish great destruction by setting fire to many mansions with his flaming tail. When he returned, Rama was overjoyed that his beloved Sita had been found and immediately made preparations to go to her rescue.

SPIRIT OF THE BUDDHA

Buddhism originated in India but spread to the countries of southeast Asia where it has become a major religious and cultural force. Buddhist thought shares with Hinduism its cosmological vision of time, including the transmigration of souls. Gautama Buddha was born in northern India in the 6th century BC. But the story of his life has become a legend which illustrates the main precepts of Buddhist thought.

The spirit of the Buddha appeared to Queen Maya of Kapilavastu in a dream: an elephant floating on a raincloud, a symbol of fertility, circled around her three times and then entered her womb. Astrologers forecast that Queen Maya and King Suddhodana would have a son who would leave the palace to become a holy man. When the baby was born, a lotus sprang from the place where he first touched the ground. Fearing that Prince Siddhartha would leave as had been prophesied, the King surrounded him with luxury. At 16 he was married to the princess Yasodhara, and 12 years later their only child Rahula was born. At about this time Siddhartha's curiosity about the outside world was aroused and he ventured outside the palace grounds. Outside, he encountered for the first time old age, sick-

LEFT *Seated Buddha in Dharmachakra attitude; (c. 1st century AD Gandhara style sculpture from Yusufzai).*

RIGHT *Gautama Buddha 'The presentation of bowls'; (relief from Buner c. 2nd – 3rd century AD Gandhara). A Buddhist monk's begging bowl is a concrete manifestation of his vow of poverty.*

ness and death and was awakened to suffering. He also met a wandering ascetic and resolved to leave his home and become a recluse. After six years of extreme asceticism he realized that he was no nearer enlightenment than he had been while living in luxury, and he resolved to follow a middle way to enlightenment, free from desire. While meditating, Siddhartha was tested by the demon Mara, first with fear and then with pleasure, but he was untouched. Eventually, he achieved insight into all his former existences. He became aware of how the terrible suffering that wastes human life is caused and how it can be eliminated, recognizing the four noble truths that became the basis of his teaching: that suffering exists; that it depends on certain conditions; that these conditions can be removed; and that the way to remove these conditions is to practise the eight-fold path – right views, right resolve, right speech, right conduct, right liveli-

hood, right effort, right mindfulness, and right concentration. Forty-nine days later he set in motion the 'wheel of teaching' by preaching his first sermon in the deer park at Sarnath. His deep sense of compassion induced him to preach for the next 45 years.

The Jataka tales are a collection of 550 stories of the former lives of the Buddha. Some of these tales are peculiarly Buddhistic, but others are evidently part of the contemporary folk lore and have been incorporated into Buddhist mythology. They give us a vivid picture of the social life and customs of ancient India. Some of these tales are quite misogynistic; women are often viewed as the source of all treachery, as in this story about a demon – or *asura* – who used to come and listen to the preaching of the Boddhisattva. The story is a moral tale which warns against hankering after worldly pleasures, although an alternative interpretation might be that it is about the wiliness of women:

BELOW *The 'Sanci torso'; red sandstone torso of a Bodhisattva from Sanci (Gupta period, 5th–9th century).*

BELOW *Stone relief representation of the great stupa at Amaravati (now destroyed) from its own casing; (Andhra Pradesh c. 150–200 AD). Buddhist stupas developed form burial mounds containing relics of the Buddha to vast representations of the cosmos and centres of Buddhist worship during the period of the Mauryan dynasty (c. 322–185 BC), when Buddhism was the imperial religion. The stupa was exported with Buddhism and in China evolved into the tiered tower pagoda.*

'WELCOME ALL THREE OF YOU'

The *asura* lived in the forest next to the highway. When he was not catching and devouring unwary travellers, the *asura* would go and listen to the teaching of the Boddhisattva. One day, he devoured the bodyguard of an exceedingly beautiful noblewoman of the area. She was so beautiful that he carried her off to his cave and took her for his wife. He brought her good things to eat, clarified butter, husked rice, fish, flesh and fresh fruit. He dressed her in rich robes and ornaments. And to keep her safe he put her in a box which he swallowed, thus guarding her in his belly.

One day, the *asura* went to the river to bathe. He threw up the box and let her out to enjoy herself in the open air while he bathed a little way off. While the *asura* was away she saw

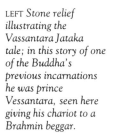

a magician flying through the air and beckoned him to her. When the magician came to her she put him into the box, covering him with her own body and wrapping her garments around him. The Asura returned and swallowed the box again, not thinking there was anyone but the woman inside it.

He decided to go and listen to the teaching of the Boddhisattva again, and as he approached, the holy man greeted him saying, 'welcome all three of you'. The *asura* was curious to know what this meant as he had come alone to visit the ascetic, and the ascetic told him that he was carrying inside his belly not only his wife but also a magician. Fearing that the magician might rip open his belly to make his escape, the *asura* threw up the box again and found his wife and the magician in the box, sporting merrily. The demon was so amazed at the Boddhisattva's vision – and so thankful that his life had been saved from the sword of the magician – that he let the woman go and praised the wisdom of the holy man:

O stern ascetic, thy clear vision saw
How low poor man, a woman's slave
    may sink;
As life itself tho' guarded in my maw,
The wretch did play the wanton, as I
    think.

I tended her with care both day and
night,
As forest hermit cherishes a flame,
And yet she sinned, beyond all sense
of right:
To do with woman needs must end in
shame.

(Jataka: *Stories of Buddha's Former
Births*, Ed. E. B. Cowell)

In other Jataka tales the Buddha is
born as an animal. In one he is a
monkey who lived alone on the river
bank. It is comparable to an Aesop's
fable where cleverness outwits force.
In Indian tales it is often the crocodile
or the tiger, the dangerous animals,
who are depicted as fools.

THE FOUR
VIRTUES

In the middle of the river was an
island on which grew many fruit
trees bearing mangoes, bread-fruit
and other good things to eat. Each
day the monkey would go to the island by jumping first onto a large rock
that stuck out of the water, using it as
a stepping stone to the island. He
would eat his fill and then return home
every evening by the same route.
Now, there was a crocodile living in
the river who was searching for food
for his pregnant wife. He determined
to catch the monkey by lying in wait
for him on the rock. On his way home
the monkey noticed that the rock was
rather higher in the river than usual
and called out 'Hi rock!' three times.
There was silence, so the wise monkey
called out, 'Why don't you speak to
me today, friend?' The foolish crocodile, thinking that the monkey was
really expecting the rock to answer
shouted out, 'It's me, the crocodile,
waiting to catch you and eat your
heart'. The crafty monkey agreed to
give himself up and told the crocodile
to open his mouth to catch him when
he jumped. As is well known, when

crocodiles open their mouths their
eyes close. So while the crocodile
could not see him the monkey used
him as his stepping stone, leaping
onto his back and then onto the bank
of the river and home. The crocodile
realized how clever the monkey had
been and said, 'Monkey, he that in
this world possesses the four virtues
overcomes his foes. And you, I think,
possess all four'. (The four virtues are
friendliness, compassion, joy and
equanimity.) Tales like these provide
endless subject matter for the sculptor
and painter, particularly as no images
of the Buddha were made at first and
he was only symbolized by a wheel,
his sandals, his stool or a Bodi-tree.
The railings of the great Buddhist
stupas at Barhut and Sanchi are teem-
ing with the characters from these
familiar tales, each one with a moral.

Muslims entered India as early as
the year 711, by the same north-
western route as the ancient Aryan
conquerors. In the 17th century the
Mughal empire, famous for its glittering court, ruled almost all of the Indian
subcontinent. Islam and Hinduism
are two very different traditions and
Islamic philosophy did not flourish as
much on Indian soil as elsewhere.
The literature of the Muslim community came more from Persian traditions. But the meeting of the two
cultures did bear fruit. There were
areas of common ground in discussion
of monism and monotheism, in the
traditions of saints, and especially in
the mystic and devotional movements
of both religions. Examples of a literature that is both Indian and Muslim
are the medieval tales of romantic
love. This 'Enchanting Story' is from
the 18th-century poet Mir Hasan:

PRINCESS
BADR I MUNIR

The beautiful young prince Benazir
was captured by a fairy named
Marhukh. She allowed him out on a

174

magic carpet each evening on condition that if he lost his heart to another he would tell her. One night on his travels he came across a group of young women by a watercourse. In the centre of the group was the 15-year-old Princess Badr i Munir, clothed in fine and delicate fabrics and adorned with pearls and other priceless jewels. When their eyes met they were both smitten with love and fell down in a swoon. Their affair developed, assisted by Badr i Munir's closest friend Najm un Nisa, until the fairy discovered it. Furious at being deceived, she imprisoned Benazir at the bottom of a dried-up well in the middle of the desert, guarded by a jinn. When Benazir came no more to their rendezvous, Badr i Munir grew sick with love and sorrow and disappointment. She lost her appetite and wandered about distracted. Crying herself to sleep one night she dreamt of Benazir and saw his plight. Her friend Najm un Nisa decided to go in search of him. Dis-

BELOW *An Indian marriage; a painting of the Mughal school from Lucknow, 1775.*

guised as an ascetic and carrying a lute, she set off. The beauty of her playing attracted the attention of Firoz Shah, the handsome son of the king of the jinns. Her own beauty shone through her disguise and captured his heart, so he carried her off to his father's palace. She stayed at court for some time, playing the lute each evening, until the prince was hopelessly in love with her and begged her to marry him. Before she would agree to his proposal she explained her mission to him and asked for his help in finding Benazir. The king of the jinns sent fairies to discover his whereabouts and rebuked Mahrukh for forming such an attachment to a human. Finally Benazir was released from his prison and brought to the palace. Firoz Shah had a magic, flying throne, and on it he carried Najm un Nisa and Benazir back to the garden of Badr i Munir. Their reunion was sweet. Their bodies weak from the sorrow of separation and their eyes red from weeping, they talked long into the night and slept late into the morning. The following day all four of them took all the necessary steps to ensure that they might be married. The weddings were celebrated with great

LEFT *Garland seller in Old Delhi; the number of festivals in India is so great that he is kept busy throughout the year. On the tenth day of the rising moon between September and October falls the most popular of Indian festivals – Dussehra – a celebration of a great victory by Rama over the Demon King Ravana. An estimated crowd of five million gathered at Uttar Pradesh for the Hindu festival of Kumbh-Mela in 1966, possibly the greatest number of human beings ever assembled with a common purpose.*

LEFT *18th-century stone sculpture of the Buddha's first sermon.*

178

pomp and ceremony, thus fulfilling the heart's desire of all four lovers.

Almost every day of the year somewhere in India a festival is held. At the most popular festivals thousands of people gather to listen to stories of their favourite heroes and gods. At the *Rama-lila,* held in Delhi in the autumn, there are theatrical performances of the great battle between Rama and Ravana, the demon king of Lanka, who kidnapped Rama's wife Sita. The performance ends with the immolation of a vast paper effigy of Ravana.

Most of the dates of the calender are marked by an event that celebrates the myths and traditions of the culture. In the villages of Maharashtra, in western India, when the new har-

vest of rice is gathered in, the villagers dance around a heap of grains with an image of a deity on top. They play a ritualistic riddle game, one half of the dancers asking the questions and the other half responding. In this way they build up a familiar story, usually out of one of the great epics. Although Indian mythology has very ancient roots, it punctuates the rhythms of everyday life and is very much alive today.

BELOW *A princess and her ladies celebrating Diwali, the festival of lights, in a palace garden, with yogis and yoginis; (a painting of the Mughal school by Hunhar, c. 1760).*

Japanese Mythology

In January 1989, Emperor Hirohito of Japan died. The enthronement ceremony of the new emperor, Akihito, was done according to Shinto tradition, for the emperor has always been the head of Japan's national religion. But opposition parties in the Japanese democracy strongly criticized the idea of employing Shinto rituals in the ceremonies concerning the funeral and the enthronement. State Shintoism is a relatively new phenomenon, started about one-and-a-half centuries ago in order to unify Japan after the long period of feudalism. It took only a few decades for this artificial state Shintoism to get out of control, and the Emperor's position as a human-god was abused, mostly by the army, to justify the invasion of neighbouring countries. It is from Shinto that the authentic Japanese mythology comes, particularly from the Kojiki, the 'Record of Ancient Things' (completed in the eighth century AD), which became a kind of statement of Shinto orthodoxy.

Paper screen by Ogata Korin (1658–1716) decorated with pink and white plum blossoms.

Traditional Shinto, as opposed to state Shintoism, has its origin about 2,000 years ago. Shinto is Japan's primal religion and is integrated into Japan's culture. Around the 3rd century BC, a Japan consisting of a single race and a single language emerged after a long period of racial and cultural diversity (though the political unification of Japan was not completed by the imperial family until the 6th century AD). Japan's birth as a nation coincided with the start of rice growing – Japan's main industry until quite recently – and Shinto consisted of rituals to pray for a good harvest, keeping the community unified through those rituals. The fact that people were primarily considered as members of the community rather than as individuals explains Shinto's survival despite of the powerful influence of Buddhism: more than 70% of the Japanese were engaged in agriculture up to the end of the Second World War.

An agricultural life is hard work, and requires activity to be coordinated with the changing seasons. This inte-

ABOVE AND BELOW
*Sections of a long
scroll painting in black
ink, 'Landscape for
Four Seasons' by
Sesshu, 1486.*

LEFT *Float decorated in
the time-honoured
tradition for the annual
Gion festival in Kyoto.*

ABOVE *Head of
Haniwa, a grave
figurine, from the 6th
century AD.*

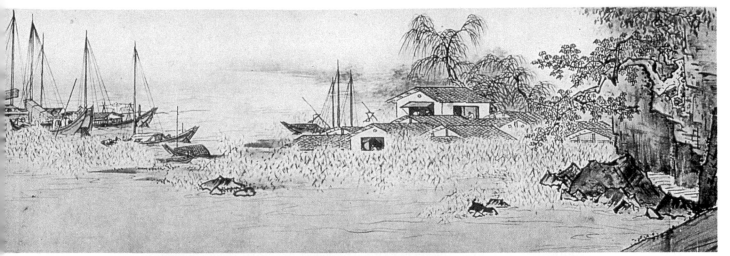

LEFT *Izumo shrine, Shimane prefecture, the oldest Shinto shrine in Japan; the Shinto gods are supposed to assemble here in October each year, thus October is termed the 'godless month' elsewhere.*

gration of people's beliefs with their working lives still exists in Japanese companies today – it is a common practice to build small Shinto shrines on top of the office buildings – but modern industrial work lacks the sensitivity to nature required for rice growing. Nature and the changing seasons were not seen as romantic or beautiful, but life was lived according to the dictates of the seasons. So not surprisingly, the concepts of virtue in Shintoism are reflected in the success, or failure, of farming. The notions of purity, or clarity, and uncleanliness, or filth, are the most fundamental concepts in Shintoism; the word *kegare* is Japanese for uncleanliness, and stems from *ke* meaning a mythical power to make things grow, and *gare* meaning lacking. Together, *kegare* therefore means a lack of power to make things grow (and particularly rice), and uncleanliness is thus associated with failure to thrive.

The main record of Shinto myth and historical legend is the *Kojiki*, the Record of Ancient Things, completed in 712 AD. Divided into three books, the first covering life with the gods, the second life with Man and the gods, and the third, Man's life without the gods. It also covers the origins of the imperial clan and the leading families. The *Kojiki* has until recently been regarded as sacred. Many of its stories involve these key concepts of purity and uncleanliness.

RIGHT *Rengyoin temple was founded in 1164 and rebuilt in 1266 after a fire. It contains 1001 small figurines of Kwannon, known in China as Guanyin, the Goddess of Mercy.*

The most popular hero in the *Kojiki* is Yamato-takeru. His story is found in Book Two, which deals with Man as he is about to depart from the world of the gods, and has the melancholic tone that characterizes so many Japanese epics:

FRATRICIDE WITHOUT REMORSE

Among the many children of Emperor Keiko were the brothers Opo-usu and Wo-usu, the second of whom was later named Yamato-takeru. One day the emperor sent Opo-usu to summon two maidens who were renowned for their beauty. But instead of summoning them, Opo-usu made them his wives and sent others in their stead. When the emperor learned of his son's betrayal, he ordered Wo-usu to persuade his elder brother to come to dine with his father. Five days passed, but Opo-usu still did not

come. When the emperor asked Wo-usu why his brother had not come, Wo-usu explained 'I captured him, grasped him, and crushed him, then pulled off his limbs, and wrapping them in a straw mat, I threw them away'.

This example of brute strength without any regard to morality explains why Yamato-takeru is seen as an embodiment of natural force, beyond the understanding of a mortal being. Nature brings about harvest, and at

BELOW *Workers in the Yamaha factory in Hamamatsu are required to take part in daily exercises, fostering the sense of being part of a community.*

185

BELOW A guardian
figure at Horyuji
temple at Nara, the
oldest preserved temple
complex in Japan and a
fine example of the
architecture of the
Asuka period
(552–645 AD).

the same time can be utterly destructive. It is to be admired and feared.

Throughout, the style of the *Kojiki* is realistic, and often cruelly bloody. This violence is in evidence throughout the adventures of Yamato-takeru as he is sent by his father the emperor to quell both real political enemies, and also 'unruly' deities. Japan's natural sport, Sumo, is characterized by its display of sheer power. Wrestlers are often very quiet people and are expected to live simply. We can see in Sumo the same sort of admiration as that shown for the boy-hero Yamato-takeru. There are many elements of Shinto ritual in Sumo. Wrestlers throw salt before each bout to purify the ring. They use water put beside the ring to clean their mouths, symbolizing the purification of the bodies. The ring is made of packed soil inside which there are various things dedicated to gods.

CLEANSING BY FIRE

Yamato-takeru next embarked on a long journey as the emperor dispatched him to destroy rebel forces.

LEFT A bout of sumo
wrestling, which may
last for a few seconds
only, ends when one of
the contestants touches
the ground with any
part of his body other
than his feet. The
reverence felt for the
explosive power of the
Sumo wrestler can be
linked to the admiration
of the mythical figure
Yamato-takeru, master
of gods and men.

First he was sent to the west to kill two mighty brothers; when he arrived at their house he found it surrounded by rows of warriors. Yamato-takeru was so young (perhaps 15 or 16) that he could disguise himself as a young girl by combing his hair down and dressing in women's clothes. He went into the house while the feast was taking place. The brothers were very pleased to see this 'girl' and had her sit between them. Then, when the feast was at its height, Yamato-takeru seized one of the brothers by the collar and stabbed him clear through the chest. The younger brother ran, but Yamato-takeru seized him and stabbed him too.

On his return home, Yamato-takeru subdued and pacified all the mountain, river and sea deities, but it was not long before the emperor commanded

LEFT Splashed-ink landscape by Sesshu, given by the artist to his pupil. The accompanying text explains how he went to China to learn this particular technique. The influence of China upon Japanese art and Japanese mythology is widespread.

ABOVE *Print by Utamaro (1754–1806) of young women visiting the seashore at Ise; at New Year the sun rises between the twin rocks, joined by a straw rope that marks the boundary of the territory of the gods.*

Yamato-takeru to deal with more unrest in the east. Yamato-takeru went to his aunt Yamato-pime, complaining that he was being sent out again too soon, and without adequate protection. On his departure, Yamato-pime gave him a sword, and a bag, and said 'Should there be an emergency, open this bag'.

Yamato-takeru, after conquering his father's enemies, met a man in the land of Sagamu who deceived him, saying that an unruly deity resided in the middle of the plain. When Yamato-takeru entered the plain, the man set fire to the area, but Yamato-takeru escaped using his aunt's bag and sword. He mowed the grass with his sword, then lit a counter-fire with a flint which he found in his aunt's bag. Then he killed the man and all his clan, burning the bodies.

One of the imperial treasures that Japan's new emperor Akihito inherited from the late Hirohito is a sword. A sword is one of the symbols of the figurehead of Shintoism, because it symbolizes lightning: thunder is re-

RIGHT *The traditional dance theatre, Kabuku, which is played by men only, has been popular since the 17th century.*

garded as promoting good harvest. The amount of thunder, and consequently rain, has most to do with the growth of rice. The idea of the gift of fire is so widespread that it would seem to be practically a part of racial memory: consider the Prometheus myth.

DEATH OF YAMATO-TAKERU

As Yamato-takeru crossed the sea, the deity of the crossing stirred up the waves, and the boat began to drift helplessly. His wife, Oto-tatiban-pime, offered to sacrifice herself to the sea god in his place, and stepped out onto layers of sedge-mats, skins and silk carpet spread out on the waves. As she went down onto them, she sang:

O you, my lord, alas –
You who once, standing among the
  flames
Of the burning fire, spoke my name
On the mountain-surrounded
Plain of Sagamu!

Seven days later, her comb was washed ashore. Taking this comb, they made

her tomb and place her within.

Yamato-takeru then experienced the first of the incidents that lead to his downfall. On his way back to the capital, when he was eating his rations at the foot of the pass of Asi-gara, the deity of the pass, assuming the form of a white deer, came and stood next to him. Yamato-takeru struck the deer with the leftovers from his meal, hitting the deer's eye and killing him. Then he climbed up the pass and, grieving, sighed three times: 'My wife, alas!'.

He is defeated by the deity of Mount Ibuki who causes a violent hail storm which dazes Yamato-takeru. His mind recovers a little as he rests at a spring, but because of his extreme fatigue he walks along slowly, using a staff. He proceeds across the plain of Tagi to the plain of Nobo, where he sings this song recalling his homeland:

> From the direction
> Of my beloved home
> The clouds are rising
> Next to the maiden's
> Sleeping place
> I left
> The sabre, the sword –
> Alas, that sword!

He dies. When his family come down to the plain of Nobo to construct his tomb, they also sing:

> The vines of the Tokoro
> Climb around
> Among the rice stems,
> The rice stems in the rice paddies
> Bordering the tomb.

The *Kojiki* has many beautiful songs such as these which anticipate *waka*, or *haiku*, Japanese poetical forms. They are symbolic rather than descriptive, their simplicity attempting to capture emotion or instantaneous thought without using words of emotion. The above song is meant to capture the desolate feeling of people who have lost the man they loved.

ABOVE *The puppets in Bunraku theatre are manipulated by three people, clearly visible behind a narrow stage.*

BELOW *Noh mask worn by an actor playing a middle-aged woman in the 15th-century drama Fukei by Tokuwaka.*

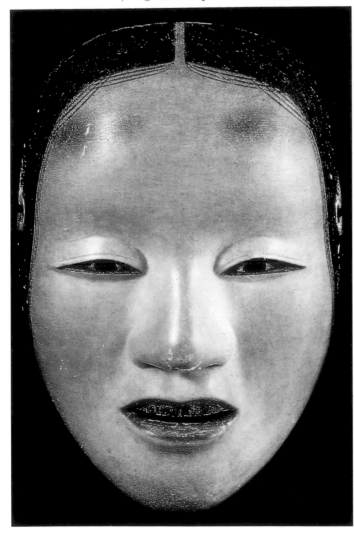

EXCLUDED FROM THE DIVINE

Transformed into a giant white bird, Yamato-takeru flew away toward the beach followed by his family:

> Moving with difficulty, up to our
>   waists
> In the field of low bamboo stalks,
> We cannot go through the skies
> but, alas, must go by foot.

As they waded into the sea, they sang:

> Going by sea, waist-deep in the
>   water
> We move forward with difficulty
> Like plants growing
> By a large river
> We drift aimlessly
> In the ocean currents.

Man from the realm of the divine, and his struggle to return, is common to many mythologies from around the world. Some authorities believe that in this tale the flight of the bird is connected to the tradition of mourners dressing as birds to sing and dance at funerals. It is either an attempt to call back the soul that has flown away, or to assist the soul in its ascent to the higher regions.

Whereas the story of Yamato-takeru deals with the story of Man, Book One of the *Kojiki* concerns itself with the creation. The cosmology of the *Kojiki* is a step-by-step evolution of the universe. There is no creation from absolute nothing by an absolute being, and the creation of the islands of Japan is described thus:

Again, when the bird had flown to the rocky shores, they sang:

> The plover of the beach
> Does not go by the beaches
> But follows along the rocky shores

These concluding songs to the story of Yamato-takeru express the destiny of earth-bound man. The exclusion of

THE BIRTH OF JAPAN

Two gods, Izanagi and Izanami, were given the command to create the islands, which they did by standing on the heavenly Floating Bridge and, lowering the heavenly Jewelled Spear, stirring with it. They stirred the brine

LEFT *The Jidai festival in Kyoto includes a 2½-mile-long procession of groups dressed in costumes representing styles from the late 8th to 19th centuries, celebrating Kyoto's time as the capital.*

191

ABOVE *When praying
at a Buddhist temple,
the devout also light
incense.*

with a churning sound: and when they lifted up the spear again, the brine dripping down from the tip of the spear piled up and became an island. Descending from the heavens, Izanagi and Izanami married on this island and erected a heavenly pillar and a spacious palace.

Discovering that their bodies were differently formed, Izanagi asked his spouse Izanami if she was agreeable to giving birth to the land. When she agreed, he suggested, 'Then let us, you and me, walk in a circle around this heavenly pillar and meet and join'. After several failures, they started to bear children, which are the islands of Japan.

There have been various interpretations of this ritual of circling around the heavenly pillar. Scholars of the late Edo period (from the 18th century to the early 19th century) regarded the pillar simply as the symbol of the phallus. It clearly has links with the European maypole, which is believed to capture the vital powers latent in a tree, and also with the ancient Japanese belief that processions round tall trees are needed to summon down the deities who live in the heavens or on high mountains.

Until the scholar Motoori Norinaga discovered the importance of the *Kojiki* in the 18th century, it was regarded as far inferior to its contemporary, the *Nihon-shoki*, a history book completed in 720AD, eight years after the presentation of the *Kojiki*. The *Nihon-shoki* is in many ways more accessible than the *Kojiki* as it presents its material in a more detached way. The *Kojiki*, on the other hand, invites the readers to have strong

BELOW *Noh drama
began in the Heian
period (8th–12th
centuries), was highly
developed by the 14th
century, and is still
very popular today.*

sympathy with the myths, and does not seem to care much about the coherence and logic of the stories it includes. Norinaga, however, thought that the very simplicity and incoherence of the *Kojiki* is what its compilers intended, aiming to recreate the religious sense of ancient Japanese through a careful organization of prose and poetry. It is important to read the myths with imagination and faith, rather than looking for rational explanations to the stories.

When the *Kojiki* was written, the influence of China was starting to be apparent everywhere. The legal system, the arts and literature were strongly affected. As the influence of Buddhism spread from China and Asia in the 6th century and became the dominant belief among the aristocracy, the *Kojiki* was important in recording Japanese life before foreign influences took too great a hold. The

book portrayed an image of life filled with a strong sense of the unity of Man with nature and god, and the unity between people through simple rituals. It also aimed to bring about clear self-consciousness through having a lucid image of the past to overcome the crisis of national identity, in some ways a crisis similar to the one Japan is facing now.

In the book, purity (or growth power) is exemplified by the story of Yamato-takeru. The opposite concept of *kaegare* (or pollution) is illustrated by the story of Izanami's death:

THE HEARTH
OF YOMI

After giving birth to numerous islands and other features of nature

BELOW Yakushi-nyorai (Lord of the Eastern Paradise) shown here flanked by two attendants in the Yakushiji temple in Nara. The gilt statues were blackened in a fire in 1528.

ABOVE RIGHT *Sacred
dance hall of Kasuge
shrine, Nara; here the
ritual Kagura dances
are performed in
honour of Amaterasu.*

– waterfalls, mountains, trees, herbs and the wind – Izanami died of a terrible fever. Izanagi followed her to Yomi, the land of the dead but was too late: she had already eaten at the hearth of Yomi. She asked Izanagi to wait for her patiently as she discussed with the gods whether she could return, but he could not. He threw down the comb he was wearing and set light to it, and then he entered the hall. What he saw was dreadful:

'Maggots were squirming and roaring in Izanami's corpse. In her head was Great-Thunder; in her breast was Fire-Thunder; in her belly was Black-Thunder; in her genitals was Crack-Thunder; in her right hand was Earth-Thunder; in her left foot was Sounding–Thunder; in her right foot was Reclining-Thunder. Altogether there were eight thunder deities.'

As can be seen from the above description of the land of the dead, ancient Japanese ideas about death and the afterlife contained no thought of a final judgement. The land of the dead, Yomi, is the land of filth and uncleanliness rather than that of horror or punishment. By eating from the hearth of Yomi, Izanami can no longer return to the land of the living. Norinaga considered that this was because food cooked with the fire of Yomi became impure. A simpler interpretation is that Izanami, having eaten the food of Yomi, had become a person of Yomi. The idea that one cannot return home after having eaten the food of the afterlife – or even of a foreign land – is a common one throughout the world. In the final passage of the relationship between Izanami and Izanagi, the concept of mortality for mankind is introduced. The use of peaches as a weapon is a sign of Chinese influence on the *Kojiki*. In China, peaches and peach trees have from antiquity been used to dispel demons and evil spirits. The peach is also often used as a symbol of longevity.

DEATH COMES
TO THE WORLD

Izanagi was frightened by the sight of Izanami, and he turned and fled. Shamed by his actions, Izanami sends the hags of Yomi to pursue him, but he evades them using magic tricks. When Izanagi arrived at the border between the land of the living and Yomi, he attacked his pursuers with three peaches he had found nearby. They all turned and fled. Then Izanagi said to the peaches: 'Just as you have

saved me, when any of the race of mortal men fall into painful straits and suffer in anguish, then do you save them also.'

Finally, Izanami herself came in pursuit of Izanagi. He pulled a huge boulder across the pass from Yomi to the land of the living, and Izanagi and Izanami stood facing each other on either side of the boulder. Izanami then said: 'O my beloved husband, if you do thus, I will each day strangle to death 1,000 of the populace of your country.' To this Izanagi replied: 'O my beloved spouse, if you do this, I will each day build 1,500 parturition huts' meaning that this number of people would be born.

Thus the marriage of Izanami and Izanagi brings the natural world into existence, and their separation, or 'divorce', is the beginning of mortality.

On his return to the land of the living, Izanagi rids himself of the sullying effects of his descent into the underworld by undergoing purification.

'He arrived at the plain by the river-mouth, where he took off his clothes and the articles worn on his body. As each item was flung on to the ground, a deity came into existence. And as Izanagi entered the water to wash himself, yet more gods were created.'

Izanagi's act of cleansing (*misogi*) shows how vital force can be recovered by purification. In the same way that rice growing follows a cycle in which both the land the the people become exhausted, and are then revitalized by water or a period of rest, so Izanagi regains his strength and vitality by taking off his heavy garments and immersing himself in the waters. Water is a potent symbol in many scenes of everyday life in Japan today. For example, as soon as you take a seat in a *sushi* restaurant in Tokyo, the table will be wiped with a white cloth soaked in water. This has little to do with hygiene, rather it is an act of purification before rice is eaten.

LEFT *Large hanging scroll painting of a waterfall by Maruyama Okyo (1733–1795), said to have been commissioned by an abbott who felt bereft without an actual waterfall to contemplate.*

LEFT *In order to make a wish come true the Japanese buy good luck Daruma dolls and paint in one of the eyes. If their wish is granted, they paint in the other as a sign of gratitude.*

RIGHT *To the untutored eye, it is very difficult to differentiate between Japanese and Chinese painting: these are in fact three of a set of eight album leaves attributed to the Chinese artist Gong Xian (fl. 1656–82), ink and slight colour on paper. Compare this to the Japanese paintings on pages 100 and 107. The long and complex relationship between the two countries has been both tragic and fruitful.*

197

Nothing evokes the feeling of clarity more for Japanese than seeing a fall of water against a mountain setting, preferably with a small shrine at the base of the waterfall.

Finally, when Izanagi washes his eyes, he brings into being three of the most important gods in the Japanese pantheon – the sun goddess, the moon god and Susano, the storm god. The brother/sister pair of Amaterasu, the sun goddess, and Tukiyomi, the moon god, are respectively responsible for day and night. Of the many stories recounted of Amaterasu, the tale of her withdrawal of labour, is very well known. Amaterasu and Susano had fallen out after Susano played a trick on the sun goddess which resulted in the destruction of her rice fields. Amaterasu retaliated by withdrawing into a cave, thus casting the world into darkness. There she stayed until a goddess, egged on by other deities, performed a riotous dance outside the cave. Unable to contain her curiosity, Amaterasu emerged and caught sight of her reflection in a mirror that the gods had suspended from a tree. Since then the world has experienced the normal cycle of day and night.

Amaterasu is supposed to be the direct ancestor of the Japanese imperial family; a mirror forms part of

BELOW *Shigisan scroll from the Kamakura period (12th–13th centuries) depicting scenes from the lives of ordinary people; agriculture, represented by the bullock, is never far away.*

the imperial regalia. The obedience
that was owed to the emperor finds an
echo in the veneration of the sun
goddess. Amaterasu occupies a key
position among the huge number of
Shinto gods (by some counts, more
than eight million) of which the
mythological creatures known as *tengu*
are amongst the most ancient.

PART HUMAN, PART BIRD

*T*engu are believed to inhabit trees
in mountainous areas, particularly
pines and cryptomerias. Part human
and part bird, they are sometimes
shown wearing cloaks of feathers or
leaves, and often sport a small, black
hat. *Tengu* love to play tricks, although
this stems more from a sense of mischief than evil. Often, however, they
fail to appreciate it when the joke is
on them! A boy taunted a *tengu* by
claiming he was able to see into heaven
by using a hollow piece of bamboo as
a telescope. The *tengu*, overcome with
curiosity, agreed to swap his cloak of
invisibility for the stick of bamboo.
When he found he had been deceived,
the *tengu* took his revenge by causing
the boy to fall into an icy river.

Oni are supposed to have come to
Japan from China along with the
Buddhist faith. They are horned devils,
often of giant size, with three fingers
and toes. Sometimes they also have
three eyes. Whereas tengu are playful,
oni are usually cruel, generally not very
bright and often lecherous, as the following stories show:

ONI AND KAPPAS

M omotaro, revered for his nobility
of spirit and accomplishments
in battle, was born into a peach. A
childless couple found the peach floating in a mountain stream, and on cut-
ting it open, revealed a tiny baby boy.
They named him Momotaro, which
means 'peach child' and brought him
up as their own son. When he was 15,
Momotaro decided to repay his
adopted parents and their neighbours
for their generosity. A number of *oni*
inhabited an island nearby and were
making raids on the mainland to steal
treasure and terrorize the population.
Taking three rice cakes from his
mother, Momotaro set off on his mission. On his way he met a dog, a

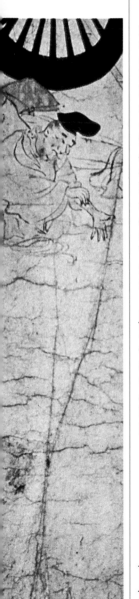

ABOVE Dotaku, *a
mysterious bronze
object, probably though
not certainly a bell,
now held by the Kobe
City Museum. Its
ritual significance or
purpose can only be
guessed at.*

pheasant and a monkey who each agreed to accompany him in return for a rice cake. The band of four took a boat to the island of the *oni*, where they found a number of girls being held captive after being kidnapped and raped. With the help of his companions, Momotaro launched an attack on the *oni* stronghold, and killed all the supernatural beings. The boat was then piled high with the stolen treasure and the prisoners released. Momotaro returned home in triumph, and was able to ensure that his parents lived out their lives in comfort.

Another diminutive hero is Issun Boshi, whose name means 'Little One Inch':

After many years of marriage, Issun Boshi's parents had not managed to conceive, so they prayed to the gods for a child, even one just as long as the end of a finger. The gods took them at their word, and Issun Boshi was born. At the age of 15 (a significant birthday for tiny heroes, it seems) Issun Boshi set off on a trip to Kyoto, the capital. He took with him his parents' gifts of a rice bowl, a pair of chopsticks and a needle stuck in a sheath of bamboo. He travelled by river, using the bowl as a boat and a chopstick as a punt. On arriving in the city, Issun Boshi found himself employment in the service of a noble family. He worked hard for a number of years and entered the affections of his employers. One day Issun Boshi accompanied the daughter of the house to the temple. On their way two giant oni leapt out in ambush. Issun Boshi tried to draw attention to himself, thus enabling the girl to escape. When one of the oni swallowed him, Issun Boshi drew his needle from its scabbard and began to stab the oni's stomach. He then clambered his way up the giant's gullet, stabbing with his weapon all the time. When he reached the mouth, the oni spat him out as fast as he could. The other oni lunged for Issun Boshi, but he jumped into its eye were he continued to wield his miniature sword.

As the hapless devils retreated, one of them dropped a mallet. Recognizing this as a lucky instrument, Issun Boshi and the girl struck it on the ground and made a wish. Immediately, Issun Boshi grew to normal size and was clothed in the armour of a samurai, whose attributes he had already shown himself to possess. On the couple's return, the father happily gave his permission for them to wed. Issun Boshi proved himself to be a devoted husband and brought his aged parents to Kyoto to share in his good fortune.

According to some, the *kappa* is a creature descended from the monkey messenger of the river god. Resembling a monkey, but with fish scales or a tortoise shell instead of fur, the child-

BELOW *Heian shrine in Kyoto; the pagoda structure is an adaptation of Chinese architecture.*

ABOVE *Picture of a* kappa *emerging from a pool; from the scroll painting* Bakemonojin, The Compendium of Ghosts *(1788).*

sized *kappa* is yellow or green in colour. They inhabit rivers, ponds and lakes and have a hollow in the top of the head in which water is carried. If this water is spilled, the *kappa* is then deprived of his magical powers. Like vampires, *kappa* feed on human blood, although they are also known to consume the blood of horses and cattle. As well as blood, *kappa* have a taste for cucumbers, and can be persuaded not to harm humans if a cucumber inscribed with the names and ages of the members of the family is thrown into the water in which they live. The ability to keep a promise is a distinguishing and appealing feature of *kappas*, as is their politeness. This is often their downfall, as when they bow down, the water spills from the indentation in the head causing their strength to disappear.

A *kappa* who resembled a small child would ask passers-by to play pull-

BELOW *Play performed at Sansen-in temple at Ohara, a mountainous area dotted with quiet villages, depicting the ancient gods and heroes.*

finger, and then drag its victims down into the pond in which it lived. A horseback rider agreed to play the game, but when their hands were locked, urged his horse into a gallop. As the water spilled from the *kappa*'s head, it begged for mercy. In return for its freedom, the *kappa* promised to teach the rider how to mend broken bones. On being released, the kappa kept its word and taught the rider all it knew. The knowledge handed over by the *kappa* was passed down through generations of the rider's family.

BUDDHIST INFLUENCE

Buddhism was introduced to Japan from Korea in the middle of the 6th century. The first, and one of the most profound texts on Buddhism, *Giso,* appeared as early as the 7th century and was written by Shotoku Taishi, a member of the imperial family who gave much support to the new religion. As is clear from the stories of the *Kojiki,* Shinto is a cult in which the spirit of every thing is worshipped, without a systematic structure or doctrine. Life after death is accepted, but early Shinto contained no moral teaching, or concept of reward or punishment after death. The term Shinto, which means 'Way of the Gods', only came into use after the introduction of Buddhism when it became necessary to differentiate between the two systems of belief.

Although there was opposition to the spread of Buddhism, by the middle of the 8th century the two religions were closely intertwined. Kobo Taishi (774–834) introduced the doctrine of Ryobu, or 'Shinto with two faces', which permitted a compromise to be reached. For the next 1,000 years, Buddhist temples would contain Shinto shrines and Shinto deities would be regarded as Buddhist guardians. Buddhist monks conducted the services at Shinto shrines (except at Izumo and Ise, where Amaterasu's shrine still exists). This happy coexistence came to an end with the beginning of the Meiji Restoration in 1868.

SOUL OF THE BUTTERFLY

This charming tale combines the Buddhist virtue of filial piety with the Shinto belief that all things, inanimate and animate, have a spirit.

A young man and woman who shared a great passion for gardening were married. They lived together in great happiness, their love for their plants only surpassed by the pleasure they took in one another's company. Late in life they had a son, who fortunately inherited his parents' interest in plants. The couple died from old age a few days apart, while their son was still a youth. The boy took over the responsibility for the garden,

ABOVE *In front of the
main building, marking
off the area of the gods,
hangs the shrine* nawa,
*which is made from
rope that has been
ritually purified.*

tending it with the care and devotion
that he had learned from his parents.
In the spring that followed their death,
he observed each day two butterflies
in the garden. One night he dreamed
that his mother and father were wandering round their beloved garden,
inspecting the plants they knew so
well to see how they were faring in
the boy's care. Suddenly, the old
couple turned into a pair of butterflies,
but continued their round of the
garden, alighting on each flower in
turn. The next day the pair of butterflies were still in the garden, and the
boy knew that they contained the
souls of his parents who were continuing to derive pleasure from their life's
work.

It was during the Kamakura period
(12th and 13th centuries) that a truly
Japanese Buddhism emerged. Honen
and his disciple Shinran were responsible for the spreading of the Jodo
school among ordinary people, and
can thus take credit for its immense
popularity ever since. Jodo made
Buddhism accessible by arguing that
one could achieve enlightenment by

abandoning oneself to Amida Buddha,
and popular Buddhism embraced
many gods, including the seven gods
of fortune.

BELOW *A* Netsuke *rat,
one of the 12 animals of
the zodiac, another of
the many examples of
Japanese borrowings
from China.* Netsuke
*are exquisitely carved
ornaments originally
used as fasteners or
brooches.*

Index

PICTURE CREDITS